Quick & Easy Recipes

Slow Cooker

Publisher's Note: Raw or semi-cooked eggs should not be consumed by babies, toddlers, pregnant or breastfeeding women, the elderly or those suffering from a chronic illness.

Publisher & Creative Director: Nick Wells
Senior Project Editor: Marcus Hardy
Art Director: Mike Spender
Layout Design: Jane Ashley
Digital Design & Production: Chris Herbert
Proofreader: Dawn Laker

Special thanks to Lydia Good for editorial and picture research assistance.

This is a **FLAME TREE** Book

FLAME TREE PUBLISHING
6 Melbray Mews, Fulham
London SW6 3NS, United Kingdom
www.flametreepublishing.com

First published 2012

Quick & Easy Recipes

Slow Cooker

FLAME TREE
PUBLISHING

Contents

Ingredients ❧

Equipment

❧

Slow cooking may be an old or completely new way of cooking for you. Either way, this book will show you everything you need to know to become an expert! This chapter will show you how to choose a cooker as well as techniques for using it. Additional information on nutrition, ingredients and using herbs and spices will set you on the road to creating tasty and nutritious slow-cooked meals.

Introducing Slow Cookers

ℭ

Most of us would love to have traditional, home-cooked food, not convenience meals or take-aways. But in today's busy world, none of us has the time or inclination to slave in the kitchen cooking all day. Welcome to the world of slow cookers. Where food tastes as it should, is tender and succulent and where, once prepared and in the pot, you can walk away and forget it. However, there are a few guidelines that are important to know before embarking on the slow-cooking way of life.

Choosing Your Cooker

It is important to take the time to ensure that the slow cooker you buy is perfect for your requirements. There are now a number of different makes and models available, which come in a large range of colours, shapes and sizes – from contemporary white and shiny stainless steel to dark, rustic earthenware or a host of eye-catching bright vibrant colours, guaranteed to brighten up any kitchen.

Types of Slow Cooker

Originally, slow cookers were only available as a round model, which were excellent for soups, stews and casseroles as well as puddings and cakes. However, slow cookers now also come in an oval shape, which is perfect for small whole fish and joints of meat such as a pot roast.

All cookers have a heat-resistant lid that is either ceramic or toughened glass; the latter is ideal for seeing what is happening without lifting the lid and losing any heat.

It is possible to get a slow cooker with a fixed inner cooking dish, but for more flexibility look for a cooker with a removable dish, referred to in this book as the 'cooking dish'.

Also, look for one where the cooking dish can be placed under the grill to brown the finished dish and can be used on the hob or even in the oven. This will save both time and effort.

Sizes of Slow Cookers

Coming in a good range of sizes, from 600 ml/1 pint to 6.5 litres/11^1/2 pints, there is a slow cooker to suit every requirement. When choosing your cooker, do think about the type of dishes you will be cooking, how many you are catering for and how often you will use your cooker.

If you feel that you would like to use the cooker nearly every day and you will be cooking for the whole family, it makes sense to buy a larger cooker than you first though of – one that you can use to its full potential.

Cooking Temperatures

All cookers have a low wattage, whatever their size. Normally, they have four settings: low, medium or auto, high and off. Cooking on high for $2^1/2$ hours is equal to 1 hour's conventional cooking. If the recipe states 'low', it can be left on low all day to cook so that your meal is waiting for you on your return with no harm done to the food. Check the instruction booklet's guidelines for suitable foods or recipes. Some cookers have a 'keep warm' setting just for this purpose; and some have a

countdown timer so that when it has finished its allotted time, it will automatically switch over to 'keep warm' until you are ready to eat.

Some foods, such as poultry, cakes and most puddings, should be cooked on high for at least the first hour, then they can be turned to auto (medium) if preferred, or according to the manufacturer's instructions or recipe guidelines.

At the low setting, the food will just simmer, which is ideal for soups and casseroles. At high, the temperature is just below boiling, so is perfect for poultry. At auto (medium), the cooker will gradually build up to high, then cook for 1 hour before automatically switching to low for the rest of the cooking time.

Care & Use of Your Slow Cooker

When using your cooker for the first time, read the handbook or instruction booklet from the manufacturer. All cookers vary, so it is important that you understand your cooker before using it.

First, remove all the packaging, then wash the cooking dish and lid in warm soapy water, rinse and dry. Always switch the cooker off on the control button and unplug after using. Empty completely and wash in soapy water, soaking if necessary to remove any stubborn food. However, do not leave the base of the cooking dish soaking in water – part of the dish is unglazed and soaking will damage it. Also, never immerse the base of the cooker itself in water. It is an electrical appliance and so the electric elements should be kept away from water. When using the cooker, stand it on a heat-resistant surface. Take care when removing tins or basins from the cooker, as they will be hot, so use oven gloves.

Cooking in Your Slow Cooker

Some slow cookers need to be preheated before use, whilst other cookers advise against heating the cooker with nothing in it, so double-check by referring to the manufacturer's instructions.

Before preheating, most manufacturers advise that a small amount of cold water, about 2.5 cm/1 inch, should be poured into the cooking dish. By doing this, when boiling water is later added, there is no harm done to the cooker through the shock of a temperature changes, as the dish is already warm. Slow cookers can be filled to within 2–3 cm/^{3}/4–1^1/4 inch of the top.

Hot or Cold Liquid?

When adding stock or other liquids, it is best to use hot but not boiling liquids; this will make the cooking process quicker than if cold liquid is used.

As we have said, never pour boiling liquid into the unheated cooking dish, as this could seriously damage the dish. Equally, never pour cold liquid into the heated cooking dish.

Food Temperature & Frozen Foods

Food should be at room temperature before being cooked in a slow cooker. All frozen foods – not only poultry, but fish and vegetables as well – must be thawed before adding to the slow cooker. This is because by adding frozen foods to the semi-cooked food in the cooker, you will drastically alter the cooking time, often prolonging it by up to 4 hours.

Puddings & Cakes

When cooking puddings or cakes, you need a trivet or upturned saucer for the basin or cake tin to stand on. Once preheated, boiling water is poured in, to come halfway up the sides of the basin or cake tin, whose top is securely covered with lightly oiled or buttered foil. Puddings and cakes are cooked on high unless the recipe states otherwise. Cooking cakes in this manner will slightly alter the texture and it is advisable, once the cake is cold, to store it in an airtight container and to eat it within 2–3 days.

Remember that, when making a cake or pudding, the colour of the raw ingredients will be the colour of the cooked dish. So, if a darker pudding or cake is preferred, use dark or light muscovado sugar. When making cakes and puddings, ensure that the dish fits. Placing a saucer or trivet in the dish will ensure that the water circulates all the way round and cooks the food evenly.

Important Points to Remember

- First – read the manufacturer's booklet and then read the recipe before starting to cook.

- Place on a heat-resistant surface, well away from the edge and from small children and pets.

- Increase the cooking time if the kitchen is cold, for example, if cooking overnight.

- Place out of draughts, as this will also affect the efficiency of the cooker.

- Ensure that any dishes used in the cooking dish will fit.

- Do not be tempted to peek; avoid lifting the lid during cooking or only do so if necessary, such as for adding more ingredients. If you do lift and peek, add an extra 15 minutes to the cooking time.

- Always use some liquid, never cook dry; so food such as baked potatoes are not suitable.

- If adapting your own recipe, use about one-third less liquid, as there is more condensation in a slow cooker.

- Take care when using alcohol; it will not evaporate as in conventional cooking.

- Ensure that the lid fits properly, otherwise the cooking time will be longer.

Using Basic Ingredients

ℰ

Compared to conventional cooking methods, using a slow cooker requires a slightly different approach to cooking basic ingredients. Because of the length of time the cooking takes there is a dangering of losing the density of more delicate foodstuffs .

∽ Cut root vegetables into small pieces, as they will take longer to cook than meat. Ensure that they are placed in the base of the dish and completely covered in liquid.

∽ Squashes, such as pumpkin, butternut or courgettes, and green vegetables take far less time to cook than root vegetables due to their higher water content, so add towards the end of the cooking time.

∽ As with conventional cooking, the long, slow cooking process suits the tougher cuts of meat very well, whereas the leaner cuts, such as fillet or sirloin steaks and chicken breast, will dry out if cooked for a very long period.

∽ When browning the meat, brown the vegetables as well. Cut the vegetables and meat into small pieces.

∽ Thicken the dish before cooking, or at the end if that is your personal preference. However, when converting one of your own recipes, use a little more thickening agent – remember this method of cooking produces more liquid.

- Season lightly at the beginning of cooking; adjust at the end of cooking.

- Whole joints and poultry should be cooked on high to ensure that any toxins and bad bacteria are destroyed.

- When using dried beans or pulses, the same rules apply as normal. Beans should be soaked overnight and those that need boiling, such as red kidney beans, will still need 10 minutes boiling to remove any toxins.

- It is better to use 'easy-cook' or parboiled rice, as the grains have more chance of not sticking together. It is a good idea to rinse the rice before using. If you cannot find 'easy-cook' rice, long-grain rice is fine to use, but rinse thoroughly.

- Both 'easy-cook' and ordinary pasta can be used; again, 'easy-cook' will give a better result. With ordinary pasta, use pasta made from 100% durum wheat, not egg pasta. Add towards the end of the cooking time.

- Sugar and dairy products do not like long, slow cooking, as they tend to break down after 6 hours. If using cream, try to stir in at the end of the cooking time rather than at the start.

- If using herbs in casseroles, stew or soups, use dry – if a recipe calls for 1 tablespoon fresh herbs, use 1 teaspoon dried herbs. Dried herbs will retain their flavour. Add fresh herbs at the end of cooking.

Using Basic Ingredients

Hygiene in the Kitchen

ℰ

I t is well worth remembering that many foods can carry some form of bacteria. In most cases, the worst it will lead to is a bout of food poisoning or gastroenteritis, although for certain people this can be more serious. The risk can be reduced or eliminated by good food hygiene and proper cooking.

Do not buy food that is past its sell-by date and do not consume any food that is past its use-by date. When buying food, use your eyes and nose. If the food looks tired, limp or a bad colour or it has a rank, acrid or simply bad smell, do not buy or eat it under any circumstances.

Do take special care when preparing raw meat and fish.

A separate chopping board should be used for each food; wash the knife, board and the hands thoroughly before handling or preparing any other food.

Regularly clean, defrost and clear out the refrigerator or freezer – it is worth checking the packaging to see exactly how long each product is safe to freeze.

Avoid handling food if suffering from an upset stomach, as bacteria can be passed on through food preparation.

Dish cloths and tea towels must be washed and changed regularly. Ideally, use disposable cloths which should be replaced on a daily basis. More durable cloths should be left to soak in bleach, then washed in the washing machine on a boil wash.

Keep the hands, cooking utensils and food preparation surfaces clean and do not allow pets to climb onto any work surfaces.

Buying

Avoid bulk buying where possible, especially fresh produce such as meat, poultry, fish, fruit and vegetables, unless buying for the freezer. Fresh foods lose their nutritional value rapidly, so buying a little at a time minimises loss of nutrients. It also eliminates a packed refrigerator, which reduces the effectiveness of the refrigeration process.

When buying prepackaged goods such as cans or pots of cream and yogurts, check that the packaging is intact and not damaged or pierced at all. Cans should not be dented, pierced or rusty. Check the sell-by dates even for cans and packets of dry ingredients such as flour and rice. Store fresh foods in the refrigerator as soon as possible – not in the car or the office.

When buying frozen foods, ensure that they are not heavily iced on the outside and the contents feel completely frozen. Ensure that the frozen foods have been stored in the cabinet at the correct storage level and the temperature is below -18°C/-0.4°F. Pack in cool bags to transport home and place in the freezer as soon as possible after purchase.

Preparation

Make sure that all work surfaces and utensils are clean and dry. Hygiene should be given priority at all times. Separate chopping boards should be used for raw and cooked meats, fish and vegetables. Currently, a variety of good-quality plastic boards come in various designs and colours. This makes differentiating easier and the plastic has the added hygienic advantage of being washable at high temperatures in the dishwasher. (NB: If using the board for fish, first wash in cold water, then in hot, to

prevent odour!) Also, remember that knives and utensils should always be thoroughly cleaned after use.

When cooking, be particularly careful to keep cooked and raw food separate to avoid any contamination. It is worth washing all fruits and vegetables, regardless of whether they are going to be eaten raw or lightly cooked. This rule should apply even to prewashed herbs and salads.

Do not reheat food more than once. If using a microwave, always check that the food is piping hot all the way through. In theory, the food should reach a minimum temperature of 70°C/158°F and needs to be cooked at that temperature for at least 3 minutes to ensure that any bacteria in the food are killed.

All poultry must be thoroughly thawed before using, including chicken and poussin. Remove the food to be thawed from the freezer and place in a shallow dish to contain the juices.

Leave the food in the refrigerator until it is completely thawed. A 1.4 kg/3 lb whole chicken will take about 26–30 hours to thaw. To speed up the process, immerse the chicken in cold water. However, make sure that the water is changed regularly. When the joints can move freely and no ice crystals remain in the cavity, the bird is completely thawed.

Once thawed, remove the wrapper and pat the chicken dry. Place the chicken in a shallow dish, cover lightly and store as close to the base of the refrigerator as possible. The chicken should be cooked as soon as possible.

Some foods can be cooked from frozen, including many prepacked foods such as soups, sauces, casseroles and breads. Where applicable, follow the manufacturers' instructions.

Vegetables and fruits can also be cooked from frozen, but meats and fish should be thawed first. The only time food can be refrozen is when the food has been thoroughly thawed, then cooked. Once the food has cooled, then it can be frozen again. On such occasions, the food can only be stored for one month.

All poultry and game (except for duck) must be cooked thoroughly. When cooked, the juices will run clear from the thickest part of the bird – the best area to try is usually the thigh. Other meats, such as minced meat and pork, should be cooked right the way through. Fish should turn opaque, be firm in texture and break easily into large flakes.

When cooking leftovers, make sure they are reheated until piping hot and that any sauce or soup reaches boiling point first.

Storing, Refrigerating & Freezing

Meat, poultry, fish, seafood and dairy products should all be refrigerated. The temperature of the refrigerator should be between 1–5°C/34–41°F, while the freezer temperature should not rise above -18°C/-0.4°F.

To ensure the optimum refrigerator and freezer temperature, avoid leaving the door open for a long time. Try not to overstock the refrigerator, as this reduces the airflow inside and affects the efficiency in cooling the food within.

When refrigerating cooked food, allow it to cool down quickly and completely before refrigerating. Hot food will raise the temperature of the refrigerator and possibly affect or spoil other food stored in it.

Food within the refrigerator and freezer should always be covered. Raw and cooked food should be stored in separate

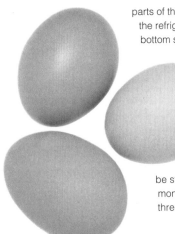

parts of the refrigerator. Cooked food should be kept on the top shelves of the refrigerator, while raw meat, poultry and fish should be placed on bottom shelves to avoid drips and cross contamination.

It is recommended that eggs should be refrigerated in order to maintain their freshness and shelf life.

Take care that frozen foods are not stored in the freezer for too long. Blanched vegetables can be stored for one month; beef, lamb, poultry and pork for six months; and unblanched vegetables and fruits in syrup for a year. Oily fish and sausages can be stored for three months. Dairy products can last four to six months, while cakes and pastries can be kept in the freezer for three to six months.

High-risk Foods

Certain foods may carry risks to people who are considered vulnerable, such as the elderly, the ill, pregnant women, babies, young infants and those suffering from a recurring illness. It is advisable to avoid those foods listed below, which belong to a higher-risk category.

There is a slight chance that some eggs carry the bacteria salmonella. Cook the eggs until both the yolk and the white are firm to eliminate this risk. Pay particular attention to dishes and products incorporating lightly cooked or raw eggs, which should be eliminated from the diet. Sauces including Hollandaise, mayonnaise, mousses, soufflés and meringues all use raw or lightly cooked eggs, as do custard-based dishes, ice creams and sorbets. These are all considered high-risk foods to the vulnerable groups mentioned above.

Certain meats and poultry also carry the potential risk of salmonella and so should be cooked thoroughly until the juices run clear and there is no pinkness left. Unpasteurised products such as milk, cheese (especially soft cheese), pâté and meat (both raw and cooked) all have the potential risk of listeria and should be avoided.

When buying seafood, buy from a reputable source which has a high turnover to ensure freshness. Fish should have bright, clear eyes, shiny skin and bright pink or red gills. The fish should feel stiff to the touch, with a slight smell of sea air and iodine. The flesh of fish steaks and fillets should be translucent, with no signs of discolouration.

Molluscs such as scallops, clams and mussels are sold fresh and are still alive. Avoid any that are open or do not close when tapped lightly. In the same way, univalves such as cockles or winkles should withdraw back into their shells when lightly prodded. When choosing cephalopods such as squid and octopus, they should have a firm flesh and pleasant sea smell.

As with all fish, whether it is shellfish or wet fish, care is required when freezing it. It is imperative to check whether the fish has been frozen before. If it has been frozen, then it should not be frozen again under any circumstances.

Hygiene in the Kitchen

Herbs ❧ Spices

The use of herbs and spices when using a slow cooker can make all the difference between a bland and a tasty dish. A variety of the most common herbs and spices, along with their uses, are listed below.

∾ Allspice – The dark allspice berries come whole or ground and have a flavour similar to that of cinnamon, cloves and nutmeg.

∾ Basil – Best fresh, but also available in dried form, basil can be used raw or cooked and works particularly well in tomato-based and Mediterranean dishes.

∾ Bay Leaves – Available in fresh or dried form as well as ground. They make up part of a bouquet garni and are particularly delicious when added to meat and poultry dishes, soups, stews, vegetable dishes and stuffing. They also impart a spicy flavour to milk puddings and egg custards.

∾ Bouquet Garni – A bouquet of fresh herbs tied with a piece of string or in a small piece of muslin. It is used to flavour casseroles, stews and stocks or sauces. The herbs that are normally used are parsley, thyme and bay leaves.

∾ Cayenne – Cayenne is the powdered form of a red chilli pepper said to be native to Cayenne. It is similar in appearance to paprika and can be used sparingly to add a fiery kick to many dishes.

~ Cardamom – Cardamom has a distinctive sweet, rich taste and can be bought whole in the pod, in seed form or ground. This sweet, aromatic spice is delicious in curries, rice, cakes and biscuits and is great served with rice pudding and fruit.

~ Chervil – Reminiscent of parsley and available either in fresh or dried form, chervil has a faintly sweet, spicy flavour and is particularly good in soups, cheese dishes, stews and with eggs.

~ Chilli – Available whole, fresh, dried and in powdered form, red chillies tend to be sweeter in taste than their green counterparts. They are particularly associated with Spanish and Mexican-style cooking and curries.

~ Chives – This member of the onion family is ideal for use when a delicate onion flavour is required. Chives are good with eggs, cheese, fish and vegetable dishes. They also work well as a garnish for soups, meat and vegetable dishes.

~ Cloves – Mainly used whole, although available ground, cloves have a very warm, sweet, pungent aroma and can be used to stud roast ham and pork, in mulled wine and punch and when pickling fruit.

~ Coriander – Coriander seeds have an orangey flavour and are particularly delicious in casseroles, curries and as a pickling spice. The leaves are used both to flavour spicy, aromatic dishes as well as a garnish.

Herbs & Spices

∽ Cumin – Available ground or as whole seeds, cumin has a strong, slightly bitter flavour. It is one of the main ingredients in curry powder and complements many fish, meat and rice dishes.

∽ Ginger – Ginger comes in many forms, but primarily as a fresh root and in dried ground form, which can be used in baking, curries, pickles, sauces and Chinese cooking.

∽ Lemongrass – Available fresh and dried, with a subtle, aromatic, lemony flavour, lemongrass is essential to Thai cooking. It is also delicious when added to soups, poultry and fish dishes.

∽ Marjoram – Often dried, marjoram has a sweet, slightly spicy flavour, which tastes fantastic when added to stuffing, meat or tomato-based dishes.

∽ Oregano – The strongly flavoured dried leaves are similar to marjoram and are used extensively in Italian and Greek cooking.

∽ Paprika – Paprika often comes in two varieties. One is quite sweet and mild and the other has a slight bite to it. Paprika is made from the fruit of the sweet pepper and is good in meat and poultry dishes as well as a garnish. The rule of buying herbs and spices little and often applies particularly to paprika, as unfortunately it does not keep especially well.

∽ Parsley – The stems as well as the leaves of parsley can be used to complement most savoury dishes, as they contain the most flavour. They can also be used as a garnish.

∽ **Pepper** – This comes in white and black peppercorns and is best freshly ground. Both add flavour to most dishes, sauces and gravies. Black pepper has a more robust flavour, while white pepper has a much more delicate flavour.

∽ **Rosemary** – The small, needle-like leaves have a sweet aroma which is particularly good with lamb, stuffing and vegetable dishes.

∽ **Saffron** – Deep orange in colour, saffron is traditionally used in paella, rice and cakes, but is also delicious with poultry.

∽ **Sage** – The fresh or dried leaves have a pungent, slightly bitter taste, which is delicious with pork and poultry, sausages, stuffing and with stuffed pasta when tossed in a little butter and fresh sage.

∽ **Savory** – This herb resembles thyme, but has a softer flavour that particularly complements all types of fish and beans.

∽ **Tarragon** – The fresh or dried leaves of tarragon have a sweet, aromatic taste, which is particularly good with poultry, seafood and fish.

∽ **Thyme** – Available fresh or dried, thyme has a pungent flavour and is included in bouquet garni. It complements many meat and poultry dishes and stuffing.

∽ **Turmeric** – This root is ground and has a brilliant yellow colour. It has a bitter, peppery flavour and is often combined for use in curry powder and mustard.

Herbs & Spices

Nutrition

𝒞

Slow cookers are useful in enabling us to find the time to provide a healthy and well-balanced diet, the body's primary energy source. In children, a healthy diet is the basis of future health and provides lots of energy. In adults, it encourages self-healing and regeneration within the body. A well-balanced, varied diet will provide the body with all the essential nutrients it needs. The ideal variety of foods is shown in the pyramid below.

Fats

Fats fall into two categories: saturated and unsaturated fats. It is very important that a healthy balance is achieved within the diet. Fats are an essential part of the diet and a source of energy and provide essential fatty acids and fat–soluble vitamins. The right balance of fats should boost the body's immunity to infection and keep muscles, nerves and arteries in good condition. Saturated fats are of animal origin and are hard when stored at room temperature. They can be found in dairy produce, meat, eggs, margarines and hard, white cooking fat (lard) as well as in manufactured products such as pies, biscuits and cakes. A high intake of saturated fat over many years has been proven to increase heart disease and high blood cholesterol levels and often leads to weight gain. The aim of a healthy diet is to keep the fat content low in the foods that we eat. Lowering the amount of saturated fat that we consume is very important, but this does not mean that it is good to consume lots of other types of fat.

Fats
milk, yogurt
and cheese
Proteins
meat, fish, poultry, eggs,
nuts and pulses

**Fruits and
Vegetables**

Starchy Carbohydrates
cereals, potatoes, bread, rice and pasta

There are two kinds of unsaturated fats: polyunsaturated fats and monounsaturated fats. Polyunsaturated fats include the following oils: safflower oil, soybean oil, corn oil and sesame oil. Within the polyunsaturated group are Omega oils. The Omega-3 oils are of significant interest because they have been found to be particularly beneficial to coronary health and can encourage brain growth and development. Omega-3 oils are derived from oily fish such as salmon, mackerel, herring, pilchards and sardines. It is recommended that we should eat these types of fish at least once a week. However, for those who do not eat fish or who are vegetarians, liver oil supplements are available in most supermarkets and health shops. It is suggested that these supplements should be taken on a daily basis. The most popular oils that are high in monounsaturates are olive oil, sunflower oil and peanut oil. The Mediterranean diet, which is based on foods high in monounsaturated fats, is recommended for heart health. Also, monounsaturated fats are known to help reduce the levels of LDL (the bad) cholesterol.

Proteins

Composed of amino acids (proteins' building bricks), proteins perform a wide variety of functions for the body, including supplying energy and building and repairing tissue. Good sources of proteins are eggs, milk, yogurt, cheese, meat, fish, poultry, nuts and pulses. (See the second level of the pyramid.) Some of these foods, however, contain saturated fats. For a nutritional balance, eat generous amounts of soya beans, lentils, peas and nuts.

Fruits and Vegetables

Not only are fruits and vegetables the most visually appealing foods, but they are extremely good for us, providing vital vitamins and minerals essential for growth, repair and protection in the human body. Fruits and vegetables are low in calories and are responsible for regulating the body's metabolic processes and controlling the composition of its fluids and cells.

🦋 Nutrition

Minerals

∾ Calcium – Important for healthy bones and teeth, nerve transmission, muscle contraction, blood clotting and hormone function. Calcium promotes a healthy heart, improves skin, relieves aching muscles and bones, maintains the correct acid-alkaline balance and reduces menstrual cramps. Good sources are dairy products, small bones of small fish, nuts, pulses, fortified white flours, breads and green, leafy vegetables.

∾ Chromium – Part of the glucose tolerance factor, chromium balances blood sugar levels, helps to normalise hunger and reduce cravings, improves lifespan, helps protect DNA and is essential for heart function. Good sources are brewer's yeast, wholemeal bread, rye bread, oysters, potatoes, green peppers, butter and parsnips.

∾ Iodine – Important for thyroid hormones and for normal development. Good sources of iodine are seafood, seaweed, milk and dairy products.

∾ Iron – As a component of haemoglobin, iron carries oxygen around the body. It is vital for normal growth and development. Good sources are liver, corned beef, red meat, fortified breakfast cereals, pulses, green, leafy vegetables, egg yolk and cocoa and cocoa products.

∾ Magnesium – Important for efficient functioning of metabolic enzymes and development of the skeleton. Magnesium promotes healthy muscles by helping them to relax and is therefore good for PMS. It is also important for heart muscles and the nervous system. Good sources are nuts, green vegetables, meat, cereals, milk and yogurt.

- **Phosphorus** – Forms and maintains bones and teeth, builds muscle tissue, helps maintain the body's pH and aids metabolism and energy production. Phosphorus is present in almost all foods.

- **Potassium** – Enables nutrients to move into cells, while waste products move out; promotes healthy nerves and muscles; maintains fluid balance in the body; helps secretion of insulin for blood sugar control to produce constant energy; relaxes muscles; maintains heart functioning and stimulates gut movement to encourage proper elimination. Good sources are fruit, vegetables, milk and bread.

- **Selenium** – Antioxidant properties help to protect against free radicals and carcinogens. Selenium reduces inflammation, stimulates the immune system to fight infections, promotes a healthy heart and helps vitamin E's action. It is also required for the male reproductive system and is needed for metabolism. Good sources are tuna, liver, kidney, meat, eggs, cereals, nuts and dairy products.

- **Sodium** – Helps to control body fluid and balance, preventing dehydration. Sodium is involved in muscle and nerve function and helps move nutrients into cells. All foods are good sources, but pickled and salted foods are richest in sodium.

- **Zinc** – Important for metabolism and the healing of wounds. It also aids ability to cope with stress, promotes a healthy nervous system and brain, especially in the growing foetus, aids bones and teeth formation and is essential for constant energy. Good sources are liver, meat, pulses, wholegrain cereals, nuts and oysters.

Nutrition

Vitamins

∽ Vitamin A – Important for cell growth and development and for the formation of visual pigments in the eye. Found in liver, meat, whole milk, red and yellow fruits and carrots.

∽ Vitamin B1 – Important in releasing energy from carbohydrate-containing foods. Good sources are yeast and yeast products, bread, fortified breakfast cereals and potatoes.

∽ Vitamin B2 – Important for metabolism of proteins, fats and carbohydrates. Found in meat, yeast extract, fortified cereals and milk.

∽ Vitamin B3 – Helps the metabolism of food into energy. Sources are milk and milk products, fortified breakfast cereals, pulses, meat, poultry and eggs.

∽ Vitamin B5 – Important for the metabolism of food and energy production. All foods are good sources, but especially fortified breakfast cereals, wholegrain bread and dairy products.

∽ Vitamin B6 – Important for metabolism of protein and fat. Vitamin B6 may also be involved with the regulation of sex hormones. Good sources are liver, fish, pork, soya beans and peanuts.

∽ Vitamin B12 – Important for the production of red blood cells and DNA. It is vital for growth and the nervous system. Good sources are meat, fish, eggs, poultry and milk.

∽ Biotin – Important for metabolism of fatty acids. Good sources of biotin are liver, kidney, eggs and nuts. Micro-organisms also manufacture this vitamin in the gut.

∾ Vitamin C – Important for healing wounds and the formation of collagen, which keeps skin and bones strong. It is an important antioxidant. Sources are fruits and vegetables.

∾ Vitamin D – Important for absorption of calcium to build bone strength. Sources are oily fish, eggs, whole milk and milk products, margarine, and sunlight – vitamin D is made in the skin.

∾ Vitamin E – Important as an antioxidant vitamin, helping to protect cell membranes from damage. Good sources are vegetable oils, margarines, seeds, nuts and green vegetables.

∾ Folic Acid – Critical during pregnancy for the development of foetus brain and nerves. It is essential for brain and nerve function and is needed for protein and red blood cell formation. Sources are wholegrain cereals, fortified cereals, green, leafy vegetables, oranges and liver.

∾ Vitamin K – Important for controlling blood clotting. Sources are cauliflower, Brussels sprouts, lettuce, cabbage, beans, broccoli, peas, asparagus, potatoes, corn oil, tomatoes and milk.

Carbohydrates

Carbohydrates come in two basic forms: starch and sugar carbohydrates. Starch carbohydrates, also known as complex carbohydrates, include cereals, potatoes, breads, rice and pasta. (See the fourth level of the pyramid). Eating wholegrain varieties also provides fibre, beneficial in preventing bowel cancer, and controlling cholesterol weight. Sugar carbohydrates, known as fast-release carbohydrates (because of the quick fix of energy they give), include sugar and sugar-sweetened products such as jams and syrups. Milk provides lactose, which is milk sugar, and fruits provide fructose, which is fruit sugar.

Soups ﾟ
Starters

Soup makes a great light lunch, starter or warming supper. These slow cooker recipes provide ample opportunity to experiment with lots of flavours. Try the Carrot and Ginger soup for simple but sophisticated entertaining or the Italian Bean Soup for a cosy night in. Starters such as Stuffed Vine Leaves are also a wonderful mealtime accompaniment or simply a tasty snack!

Curried Parsnip Soup

Serves 4

1 tsp cumin seeds
2 tsp coriander seeds
1 tsp oil
1 onion, peeled and chopped
1 garlic clove, peeled
and crushed
$1/2$ tsp turmeric
$1/4$ tsp chilli powder
1 cinnamon stick
450 g/1 lb parsnips, peeled
and chopped
1 litre/1$3/4$ pints
vegetable stock
salt and freshly ground
black pepper
2–3 tbsp low-fat natural yogurt, to serve
fresh coriander leaves,
to garnish

In a small frying pan, dry-fry the cumin and coriander seeds over a moderately high heat for 1–2 minutes, shaking the pan during cooking, until the seeds are lightly toasted. Reserve until cooled, then grind the toasted seeds in a pestle and mortar.

Heat the oil in a saucepan. Cook the onion until softened and starting to turn golden. Add the garlic, turmeric, chilli powder and cinnamon stick to the pan. Continue to cook for a further minute.

Add the parsnips and stir well. Pour in the stock and bring to the boil. Transfer to the cooking dish and cover with the lid. Switch to low and cook for 6–8 hours.

Allow the soup to cool. Once cooled, remove the cinnamon stick and discard. Blend the soup in a food processor until very smooth.

Return to the cooking dish and switch to high. Cover with the lid and cook for 30 minutes or until piping hot. Season to taste with salt and pepper. Garnish with fresh coriander and serve immediately with the yogurt.

Tomato ✢ Basil Soup

Serves 4

1.1 kg/2¹/₂ lb ripe tomatoes,
cut in half
2 garlic cloves
1 tsp olive oil
1 tbsp balsamic vinegar
1 tbsp dark brown sugar
1 tbsp tomato purée
300 ml/¹/₂ pint vegetable stock
6 tbsp low-fat natural yogurt
2 tbsp freshly chopped basil
salt and freshly ground
black pepper
small basil leaves, to garnish

Preheat the oven to 200˚C/400˚F/Gas Mark 6. Evenly spread the tomatoes and unpeeled garlic in a single layer in a large roasting tin.

Mix the oil and vinegar together. Drizzle over the tomatoes and sprinkle with the dark brown sugar. Roast the tomatoes in the preheated oven for 20 minutes until tender and lightly charred in places.

Remove from the oven and allow to cool slightly. When cool enough to handle, squeeze the softened flesh of the garlic from the papery skin.

Place with the charred tomatoes in a nylon sieve over a saucepan. Press the garlic and tomatoes through the sieve with the back of a wooden spoon. When all the flesh has been sieved, add the tomato purée and vegetable stock.

Transfer to the cooking dish and cover with the lid. Switch to high and cook for 2 hours. Reduce the heat to low and cook for a further 3 hours. In a small bowl, beat the yogurt and basil together and season to taste with salt and pepper. Stir the basil yogurt into the soup. Garnish with basil leaves and serve immediately.

Tuna Chowder

Serves 4

2 tsp oil
1 onion, peeled and
finely chopped
2 celery stalks, trimmed and finely sliced
1 tbsp plain flour
600 ml/1 pint skimmed milk
200 g can tuna in water
320 g can sweetcorn in water, drained
2 tsp freshly chopped thyme
salt and freshly ground
black pepper
pinch cayenne pepper
2 tbsp freshly chopped parsley

Heat the oil in a large, heavy-based saucepan. Add the onion and celery and cook gently for about 5 minutes, stirring from time to time, until the onion is softened. Stir in the flour and cook for about 1 minute to thicken.

Draw the pan off the heat and gradually pour in the milk, stirring throughout. Transfer to the cooking dish.

Add the tuna and its liquid, the drained sweetcorn and the thyme. Stir gently. Cover with the lid and switch to high. Cook for 1 hour, then reduce the heat to low and cook for a further 4–5 hours.

Stir well and season to taste with salt and pepper. Sprinkle the chowder with the cayenne pepper and chopped parsley. Divide into soup bowls and serve immediately.

Carrot ✤ Ginger Soup

Serves 4

4 slices bread,
crusts removed
1 tsp yeast extract
2 tsp olive oil
1 onion, peeled and chopped
1 garlic clove, peeled
and crushed
1/2 tsp ground ginger
450 g/1 lb carrots, peeled
and chopped
1 litre/1 3/4 pints vegetable stock
2.5 cm/1 inch piece root ginger, peeled
and finely grated
salt and freshly ground
black pepper
1 tbsp lemon juice

To garnish
chives
lemon zest

Preheat the oven to 180°C/350°F/Gas Mark 4. Roughly chop the bread. Dissolve the yeast extract in 2 tablespoons warm water and mix with the bread.

Spread the bread cubes over a lightly oiled baking tray and bake for 20 minutes, turning halfway through. Remove from the oven and reserve.

Heat the oil in a large saucepan. Gently cook the onion and garlic for 3–4 minutes. Stir in the ground ginger and cook for 1 minute to release the flavour. Add the chopped carrots, then stir in the stock and the fresh ginger. Bring to the boil.

Transfer to the cooking dish. Cover with the lid and switch to low. Cook for 6–8 hours.

Remove from the heat and allow to cool a little. Blend until smooth, then season to taste with salt and pepper. Stir in the lemon juice. Garnish with the chives and lemon zest and serve immediately.

Potato ❧ Fennel Soup

Serves 4

25 g/1 oz butter
2 large onions, peeled and
thinly sliced
2–3 garlic cloves,
peeled and crushed
1 tsp salt
2 medium potatoes (about 450 g/
1 lb in weight), peeled
and diced
1 fennel bulb, trimmed and finely
chopped
$1/2$ tsp caraway seeds
1 litre/$1^3/4$ pints
vegetable stock
freshly ground black pepper
2 tbsp freshly chopped parsley
4 tbsp crème fraîche
roughly torn pieces of French stick,
to serve

Melt the butter in a large, heavy-based saucepan. Add the onions with the garlic and half the salt and cook over a medium heat, stirring occasionally, for 7–10 minutes until the onions are very soft and beginning to turn brown.

Add the potatoes, fennel bulb, caraway seeds and the remaining salt. Cook for about 5 minutes, then pour in the vegetable stock. Transfer to the cooking dish. Switch to high and cook for 2 hours. Switch to auto and cook for 2 hours or reduce the heat to low and cook for a further 4–5 hours. Stir in the chopped parsley and adjust the seasoning to taste.

For a smooth-textured soup, allow to cool slightly, then pour into a food processor or blender and blend until smooth. Reheat the soup on low for 1 hour, then ladle into individual soup bowls. For a chunky soup, omit this blending stage and ladle straight from the cooking dish into soup bowls.

Swirl a spoonful of crème fraîche into each bowl and serve immediately with roughly torn pieces of French stick.

Rice ❧ Tomato Soup

Serves 4

150 g/5 oz easy-cook
basmati rice
400 g can chopped tomatoes
2 garlic cloves, peeled
and crushed
grated zest of 1/2 lime
2 tbsp extra virgin olive oil
1 tsp sugar
salt and freshly ground
black pepper
300 ml/1/2 pint vegetable stock
or water

For the croutons

2 tbsp prepared pesto sauce
2 tbsp olive oil
6 thin slices ciabatta bread, cut
into 1 cm/1/2 inch cubes

Preheat the oven to 220°C/425°F/Gas Mark 7. Rinse and drain the basmati rice. Place the canned tomatoes with their juice into the cooking dish and add the garlic, lime zest, oil and sugar. Season to taste with salt and pepper. Cover with the lid and switch the cooker to high. Cook for 1 hour.

Add the vegetable stock or water and the rice to the dish. Switch to auto and cook for 3 hours, or reduce the heat to low and continue to cook for a further 5 hours, or until the rice is tender. If the soup is too thick, add a little more water. Reserve and keep warm if the croutons are not ready.

Meanwhile, to make the croutons, mix the pesto and olive oil in a large bowl. Add the bread cubes and toss until they are coated completely with the mixture. Spread onto a baking sheet and bake in the preheated oven for 10–15 minutes until golden and crisp, turning them over halfway through cooking. Serve the soup immediately, sprinkled with the warm croutons.

Bread 🐝 Tomato Soup

Serves 4

900 g/2 lb very ripe tomatoes
4 tbsp olive oil
1 onion, peeled and
finely chopped
1 tbsp freshly chopped basil
3 garlic cloves, peeled
and crushed
¼ tsp hot chilli powder
salt and freshly ground
black pepper
600 ml/1 pint vegetable or chicken stock
175 g/6 oz stale white bread
50 g/2 oz cucumber, cut into small dice
4 whole basil leaves

Make a small cross in the base of each tomato, then place in a bowl and cover with boiling water. Allow to stand for 2 minutes, or until the skins have started to peel away, then drain, remove the skins and seeds and chop into large pieces.

Heat 3 tablespoons of the olive oil in a saucepan and gently cook the onion until softened. Add the skinned tomatoes, chopped basil, garlic and chilli powder and season to taste with salt and pepper. Transfer to the cooking dish. Pour in the stock, cover with the lid and switch to high. Cook for 1 hour. Switch to auto for 2 hours, or reduce the heat to low and continue to cook for a further 3 hours.

Remove the crusts from the bread and break into small pieces. Stir the bread into the tomato mixture. Cover and leave to stand for 10 minutes, or until the bread has blended with the tomatoes. Season to taste and stir well. Serve warm or cold with a swirl of olive oil on the top, garnished with a spoonful of chopped cucumber and basil leaves.

Italian Bean Soup

Serves 4

2 tsp olive oil
1 leek, washed and chopped
1 garlic clove, peeled
and crushed
2 tsp dried oregano
75 g/3 oz green beans, trimmed
and cut into bite-size pieces
410 g can cannellini beans, drained
and rinsed
1 litre/1¾ pints vegetable stock
75 g/3 oz small pasta shapes
8 cherry tomatoes
salt and freshly ground
black pepper
3 tbsp freshly shredded basil

Heat the oil in a large saucepan. Add the leek, garlic and oregano and cook gently for 5 minutes, stirring occasionally. Stir in the green beans and the cannellini beans and pour in the stock. Bring to the boil.

Transfer to the cooking dish and cover with the lid. Switch to high. Cook for 1 hour, then reduce the heat to low and cook for a further 5–6 hours.

Sprinkle in the pasta and cook for a further 30 minutes, or until the vegetables are tender and the pasta is cooked to *al dente*, stirring occasionally.

In a heavy-based frying pan, dry-fry the tomatoes over a high heat until they soften and the skins begin to blacken.

Gently crush the tomatoes in the pan with the back of a spoon and add to the soup. Season to taste with salt and pepper. Stir in the shredded basil and serve immediately.

Bacon ❧ Split Pea Soup

Serves 4

50 g/2 oz dried split peas
25 g/1 oz butter
1 garlic clove, peeled and finely chopped
1 medium onion, peeled and thinly sliced
175 g/6 oz easy-cook long-
grain rice
2 tbsp tomato purée
175 g/6 oz carrots, peeled and finely diced
1.1 litres/2 pints vegetable or chicken stock
125 g/4 oz streaky bacon,
finely chopped
salt and freshly ground
black pepper
2 tbsp freshly chopped parsley
4 tbsp single cream
warm crusty garlic bread,
to serve

Cover the dried split peas with plenty of cold water, cover loosely and leave to soak for a minimum of 12 hours, or preferably overnight.

Melt the butter in a heavy-based saucepan, add the garlic and onion and cook for 2–3 minutes, without colouring. Add the rice, drained split peas, tomato purée and carrots. Cook for 2–3 minutes, stirring constantly to prevent sticking. Slowly pour in the stock, then transfer to the cooking dish and cover with the lid. Switch the slow cooker to high and cook for 2 hours. Reduce the heat to low and cook for a further 4 hours.

Cool slightly, then carefully blend about three quarters of the soup in a food processor or blender to form a smooth purée. Return the purée to the soup left in the slow cooker. Cook on low for 1 hour, or until piping hot. Meanwhile, place the bacon in a nonstick frying pan and cook over a gentle heat until the bacon is crisp. Remove and drain on absorbent kitchen paper. Season the soup with salt and pepper to taste, then stir in the parsley and cream. Ladle into soup bowls. Sprinkle with the bacon and serve immediately with warm garlic bread.

Stuffed Vine Leaves

Serves 6–8

150 g/5 oz easy-cook
long-grain rice
225 g/8 oz fresh or preserved
vine leaves
225 g/8 oz red onion, peeled
and finely chopped
3 baby leeks, finely sliced
25 g/1 oz freshly chopped parsley
25 g/1 oz freshly chopped mint
25 g/1 oz freshly chopped dill
150 ml/¼ pint extra virgin olive oil
salt and freshly ground
black pepper
50 g/2 oz currants
50 g/2 oz ready-to-eat dried apricots,
finely chopped
25 g/1 oz pine nuts
juice of 1 lemon
600–750 ml/1–1¼ pints hot stock
lemon wedges or slices, to garnish
4 tbsp Greek-style yogurt, to serve

Soak the rice in cold water for 30 minutes. If using fresh vine leaves, blanch 5–6 leaves at a time in salted boiling water for 1 minute. Rinse and drain. If using preserved vine leaves, soak in tepid water for at least 20 minutes, drain, rinse and pat dry with absorbent kitchen paper.

Mix the onion and leeks with the herbs and half the oil. Add the drained rice, mix and season to taste with salt and pepper. Stir in the currants, apricots, pine nuts and lemon juice. Spoon 1 teaspoon of the filling at the stalk end of each leaf. Roll, tucking the side flaps, not too tightly, into the centre to create a parcel.

Layer half the remaining vine leaves over the base of the cooking dish. Pack the little parcels in the cooking dish and cover with the remaining leaves. Pour in enough stock to cover the vine leaves, add a pinch of salt and switch to high. Cook for 1 hour, then reduce the heat to auto and cook for a further 2 hours, or until the rice is tender. Leave to stand for 10 minutes. Using a slotted draining spoon, remove from the slow cooker and arrange on a serving dish. Garnish with lemon wedges and serve hot with the Greek yogurt.

White Bean Soup

§

Serves 4

3 thick slices white bread, cut into
1 cm/¹/₂ inch cubes
3 tbsp groundnut oil
2 tbsp Parmesan cheese,
finely grated
1 tbsp light olive oil
1 large onion, peeled and
finely chopped
50 g/2 oz unsmoked bacon
lardons (or thick slices
bacon, diced)
1 tsp dried thyme leaves
2 x 400 g cans cannellini
beans, drained
900 ml/1¹/₂ pints chicken stock
salt and freshly ground
black pepper
1 tbsp prepared pesto sauce
50 g/2 oz piece pepperoni
sausage, diced
1 tbsp fresh lemon juice
1 tbsp fresh basil,
roughly shredded

Preheat the oven to 200°C/400°F/Gas Mark 6. Place the cubes of bread in a bowl and pour over the groundnut oil. Stir to coat the bread, then sprinkle over the Parmesan cheese. Place on a lightly oiled baking tray and bake in the preheated oven for 10 minutes, or until crisp and golden.

Heat the olive oil in a large saucepan and cook the onion for 4–5 minutes until softened. Add the bacon and thyme and cook for a further 3 minutes. Stir in the beans, stock and black pepper, then transfer to the cooking dish. Cover with the lid and switch to high. Cook for 1 hour, then reduce the heat to low and cook for a further 4 hours. Switch the cooker off and leave for 20 minutes to cool. Place half the bean mixture and liquid into a food processor and blend until smooth.

Return the purée to the cooking dish. Stir in the pesto sauce, pepperoni sausage and lemon juice and season to taste with salt and pepper.

Switch the slow cooker to high. Cook for a further 1 hour, or until piping hot. Ladle the soup into serving bowls. Garnish with shredded basil and serve immediately with the croutons scattered over the top.

Mushroom & Red Wine Pâté

Serves 4

3 large slices white bread,
crusts removed
2 tsp oil
1 small onion, peeled and
finely chopped
1 garlic clove, peeled
and crushed
350 g/12 oz button mushrooms,
wiped and finely chopped
150 ml/¼ pint red wine
½ tsp dried mixed herbs
1 tbsp freshly chopped parsley
salt and freshly ground
black pepper
2 tbsp low-fat cream cheese

To serve

finely chopped cucumber
finely chopped tomato

Preheat the oven to 180°C/350°F/Gas Mark 4. Cut the bread in half diagonally. Place the bread triangles on a baking tray and cook for 10 minutes.

Remove from the oven and split each bread triangle in half to make 12 triangles and return to the oven until golden and crisp. Leave to cool on a wire rack.

Heat the oil in a saucepan and gently cook the onion and garlic until transparent. Add the mushrooms and cook, stirring, for 3–4 minutes until the mushroom juices start to run.

Stir the wine and herbs into the mushroom mixture and bring to the boil. Transfer to the cooking dish. Cover with the lid and switch to high. Cook for 1 hour, then reduce to low and cook for a further 1 hour.

Switch the slow cooker off and season the mixture to taste with salt and pepper. Leave to cool. When cold, place the mushrooms in a bowl and beat in the soft cream cheese and adjust the seasoning. Place in a small, clean bowl and chill until required. Serve with the toast triangles, the cucumber and tomato.

Fish ❧ Seafood

Fish and seafood offer a wealth of choices: from casserole to curry, baked fish to creamy risotto. The slow cooker will help you to create delicious dishes such as Smoked Haddock Kedgeree or Coconut Fish Curry with ease. Alternatively, try a vegetable dish of Ratatouille and Mackerel or impress your friends with the Mediterranean taste of Squid with Romesco Sauce.

Smoked Haddock Kedgeree

ご

Serves 4

50 g/2 oz butter
450 g/1 lb smoked haddock fillets
1 onion, peeled and finely chopped
2 tsp mild curry powder
175 g/6 oz easy-cook
long-grain rice
450 ml/³⁄4 pint fish or vegetable stock, heated
2 large eggs, hard-boiled and shelled
2 tbsp freshly chopped parsley
2 tbsp whipping cream (optional)
salt and freshly ground
black pepper
pinch cayenne pepper

Use a little of the butter to lightly grease the cooking dish. Place the haddock in the dish and pour in 300 ml/½ pint water. Cover with the lid and switch the cooker to high. Cook for 30 minutes, or until tender. Take the fish out and place on a board. Remove all the skin and bones from the fish and flake into a dish. Reserve.

Meanwhile, melt the remaining butter in a saucepan and add the chopped onion and curry powder. Cook, stirring, for 3–4 minutes until the onion is soft, then stir in the rice. Cook for a further minute, stirring continuously, then stir in the hot stock.

Transfer to the cleaned cooking dish and switch to high. Cover with the lid and cook for 40 minutes, or until the rice is almost tender. Add the fish and cook for a further 40 minutes, or until the rice has absorbed all the liquid. Cut the eggs into quarters or eighths and add half to the mixture with half the parsley.

Carefully stir in the cream, if using. Season to taste with salt and pepper. Heat the kedgeree for a further 15 minutes, or until piping hot. Transfer the mixture to a large dish and garnish with the remaining eggs and parsley. Serve immediately with a pinch of cayenne pepper.

Hot Salsa-filled Sole

Serves 4

8 x 175 g/6 oz lemon
sole fillets, skinned
150 ml/¼ pint orange juice
2 tbsp lemon juice

For the salsa
1 small mango
8 cherry tomatoes, quartered
1 small red onion, peeled
and finely chopped
pinch sugar
1 red chilli
2 tbsp rice vinegar
zest and juice of 1 lime
1 tbsp olive oil
sea salt and freshly ground black pepper
2 tbsp freshly chopped mint
lime wedges, to garnish
salad leaves, to serve

First, make the salsa. Peel the mango and cut the flesh away from the stone. Chop finely and place in a small bowl. Add the cherry tomatoes to the mango together with the onion and sugar.

Cut the top off the chilli. Slit down the side and discard the seeds and the membrane (the skin to which the seeds are attached). Finely chop the chilli and add to the mango mixture with the vinegar, lime zest, juice and oil. Season to taste with salt and pepper. Mix thoroughly and leave to stand for 30 minutes to allow the flavours to develop.

Lay the fish fillets on a board, skinned side up, and pile the salsa on the tail end of the fillets. Fold the fillets in half, season and place in the cooking dish. Pour over the orange and lemon juice. Place the dish in the slow cooker and cover with the lid.

Switch the cooker to high and cook for 30 minutes. Check that the orange and lemon juice has not evaporated and, if necessary, add 3–4 tablespoons more juice or water. Switch the cooker to low and continue to cook for 30 minutes, or until the fish is opaque. Garnish with lime wedges and mint and serve immediately with the salad.

Ratatouille ❧ Mackerel

Serves 4

1 red pepper
1 tbsp olive oil
1 red onion, peeled
1 garlic clove, peeled and thinly sliced
2 courgettes, trimmed and
cut into thick slices
400 g can chopped tomatoes
sea salt and freshly ground
black pepper
4 x 275 g/10 oz small mackerel,
cleaned and heads removed
spray of olive oil
lemon juice, for drizzling
12 fresh basil leaves
couscous or rice mixed with
chopped basil or parsley, to serve

Cut the top off the red pepper, remove the seeds and membrane, then cut into chunks. Cut the red onion into thick wedges.

Heat the oil in a large pan and cook the onion and garlic for 5 minutes, or until beginning to soften. Add the pepper chunks and courgette slices and cook for a further 5 minutes.

Pour in the chopped tomatoes with their juice and cook for a further 5 minutes. Season to taste with salt and pepper and spoon into the cooking dish.

Season the fish with salt and pepper and arrange on top of the vegetables. Spray with a little olive oil and drizzle with lemon juice. Cover the slow cooker with the lid and switch to high. Cook for 1 hour.

Switch off the cooker, then sprinkle over the basil leaves. Leave to stand for 10 minutes to allow the vegetables and fish to finish cooking and to absorb the flavour from the basil. Serve with couscous or rice mixed with freshly chopped basil or parsley.

Whole-baked Fish

Serves 8

1.25 kg/2¹/₂ lb whole salmon trout
or small salmon, cleaned
sea salt and freshly ground black pepper
50 g/2 oz low-fat spread
1 garlic clove, peeled and finely sliced
grated zest and juice of 1 lemon
grated zest of 1 orange
1 tsp freshly grated nutmeg
3 tbsp Dijon mustard
2 tbsp fresh white breadcrumbs
2 bunches fresh dill
1 bunch fresh tarragon
1 lime, sliced
150 ml/¹/₄ pint half-fat
crème fraîche
450 ml/³/₄ pint fromage frais
dill sprigs and lime or orange slices,
to garnish

Lightly rinse the fish and dry with absorbent kitchen paper. Season the cavity with salt and pepper. Make diagonal cuts across the flesh of the fish and season. Mix together the low-fat spread, garlic, lemon and orange zest and lemon juice, nutmeg, mustard and fresh breadcrumbs.

Spoon the breadcrumb mixture into the slits along with a small sprig of dill. Place the remaining herbs inside the fish cavity. Lay the fish on a double thickness of nonstick baking paper. If liked, smear the fish with a little low-fat spread. Top with the lime slices and fold the paper into a parcel.

Place in the cooking dish and switch to high. Cover with the lid and cook for 30 minutes, then switch to auto and continue cooking for 2 hours, or reduce the heat to low and cook for 3–4 hours until the fish is cooked. (You will need a large slow cooker to cook a whole fish of this size. Otherwise, cut off the head and tail before cooking.) To test if the fish is cooked, insert a skewer into the thickest part of the fish; if it yields easily with no resistance, it is cooked.

Remove the fish from the cooker and leave it to stand for 10 minutes. Stir the crème fraîche and fromage frais into the fish juices in the dish. Switch to high and cook for 15–20 minutes, stirring occasionally. Garnish and serve immediately.

Coconut Fish Curry

Serves 4

2 tbsp sunflower oil
1 medium onion, very finely chopped
1 yellow pepper, deseeded
and chopped
1 garlic clove, peeled and crushed
1 tbsp mild curry paste
2.5 cm/1 inch piece root ginger,
peeled and grated
1 red chilli, deseeded and chopped
400 ml can coconut milk
700 g/1½ lb chunks skinned, firm white fish,
e.g. monkfish
225 g/8 oz basmati rice
1 tbsp freshly chopped coriander

To garnish
lime wedges
fresh coriander sprigs

To serve
mango chutney
Greek yogurt
warm naan bread

Put 1 tablespoon of the oil into a large saucepan and cook the onion, pepper and garlic for 5 minutes, or until soft. Add the remaining oil, curry paste, ginger and chilli and cook for a further minute.

Pour in the coconut milk and bring to the boil. Stir in the fish, then transfer to the cooking dish.

Sprinkle in the rice and cover with the lid. Cook on high for 1 hour, then switch to auto and cook for a further 30–40 minutes until the fish and rice are tender.

Spoon the curry and rice into a serving dish and sprinkle with the chopped coriander. Garnish with lime wedges and coriander sprigs and serve immediately with the chutney, spoonfuls of Greek yogurt and warm naan bread.

Cod with Fennel & Cardamom

Serves 4

1 garlic clove, peeled and crushed
finely grated zest of 1 lemon
1 tsp lemon juice
1 tbsp olive oil
1 fennel bulb
1 tbsp cardamom pods
salt and freshly ground
black pepper
4 x 175 g/6 oz thick cod fillets

Place the garlic in a small bowl with the lemon zest, juice and olive oil and stir well. Cover and leave to infuse for at least 30 minutes. Stir well before using.

Trim the fennel bulb, slice thinly and place in a bowl. Place the cardamom pods in a pestle and mortar and lightly pound to crack the pods. Alternatively, place in a polythene bag and pound gently with a rolling pin. Add the crushed cardamom to the fennel slices.

Season the fish with salt and pepper and place onto four separate 20.5 x 20.5 cm/8 x 8 inch baking parchment squares. Spoon the fennel mixture over the fish and drizzle with the infused oil.

Place the parcels in the cooking dish. Cover with the lid and switch to high. Cook on high for 30 minutes, then switch to auto and cook for a further 30 minutes, or reduce to low and cook for 1 hour, or until the fish is opaque. Serve immediately in the paper parcels.

Chunky Halibut Casserole

Serves 6

50 g/2 oz butter or margarine
2 large onions, peeled and sliced into rings
1 red pepper, deseeded
and roughly chopped
450 g/1 lb potatoes, peeled
450 g/1 lb courgettes, trimmed
and thickly sliced
2 tbsp plain flour
1 tbsp paprika
2 tsp vegetable oil
300 ml/½ pint white wine
150 ml/¼ pint fish stock
400 g can chopped tomatoes
2 tbsp freshly chopped basil
salt and freshly ground
black pepper
450 g/1 lb halibut fillet, skinned and cut into
2.5 cm/1 inch cubes
fresh basil sprigs, to garnish
freshly cooked rice, to serve

Melt the butter or margarine in a large saucepan, add the onions and pepper and cook for 5 minutes, or until softened.

Cut the peeled potatoes into 2.5 cm/1 inch dice, rinse lightly and shake dry, then add them with the onions and pepper to the pan together with the courgettes.

Sprinkle the flour, paprika and vegetable oil into the saucepan and cook, stirring continuously, for 1 minute. Transfer to the cooking dish. Pour in 150 ml/¼ pint of the wine with all the stock and the chopped tomatoes, and cover with the lid.

Switch to high and cook for 1 hour. Add the basil to the cooking dish, season to taste with salt and pepper and cover with the lid. Continue to cook for a further 30 minutes before adding the halibut and the remaining wine. Switch to auto and cook for 1 hour, or reduce the heat to low and cook for 3–4 hours until the fish and vegetables are just tender. Garnish with basil sprigs and serve immediately with freshly cooked rice.

Seafood Risotto

Serves 4

50 g/2 oz butter
2 shallots, peeled and
finely chopped
1 garlic clove, peeled
and crushed
300 g/10 oz easy-cook or
Arborio rice
150 ml/¼ pint white wine
600 ml/1 pint fish or vegetable
stock, heated
125 g/4 oz large,
unpeeled prawns
290 g can baby clams
50 g/2 oz smoked
salmon trimmings
2 tbsp freshly chopped parsley

To serve
green salad
crusty bread
Parmesan cheese

Melt the butter in a large, heavy-based saucepan, add the shallots and garlic and cook for 2 minutes until slightly softened. Add the rice and cook for 1–2 minutes, stirring continuously, then pour in the wine and boil for 1 minute.

Gradually pour in all the hot fish or vegetable stock, then bring to the boil. Carefully transfer to the cooking dish. Cover with the lid and switch the slow cooker to high. Cook for 1 hour.

Meanwhile, prepare the fish by peeling the prawns and removing the heads and tails. Drain the clams and discard the liquid. Cut the smoked salmon trimmings into thin strips.

When the rice has cooked, stir in the prawns, clams, smoked salmon strips and half the chopped parsley. Switch to auto and cook for 30 minutes or until everything is piping hot. Turn into a serving dish, sprinkle with the remaining parsley and the Parmesan cheese and serve immediately with the green salad and crusty bread.

Squid with Romesco Sauce

Serves 4

8 small squid, about 350 g/12 oz
3 tbsp olive oil
50 g/2 oz pancetta, diced
1 onion, peeled and chopped
3 garlic cloves, peeled and
finely chopped
1 tsp dried thyme
50 g/2 oz sun-dried
tomatoes in oil, drained
and chopped
75 g/3 oz fresh white breadcrumbs
2 tbsp freshly chopped basil
juice of ½ lime
salt and freshly ground
black pepper
2 vine-ripened tomatoes, peeled
and finely chopped
pinch dried chilli flakes
1 tsp dried oregano
1 large red pepper, skinned
and chopped
assorted salad leaves,
to serve

Clean the squid, rinse lightly, pat dry with absorbent kitchen paper and finely chop the tentacles. Heat 1 tablespoon of the olive oil in a large, nonstick frying pan and fry the pancetta for 5 minutes, or until crisp. Remove the pancetta and reserve. Add the tentacles, onion, 2 garlic cloves, thyme and sun-dried tomatoes to the oil remaining in the pan and cook gently for 5 minutes, or until softened.

Remove the pan from the heat and stir in the diced pancetta. Blend in a food processor if a smoother stuffing is preferred, then stir in the breadcrumbs, basil and lime juice. Season to taste with salt and pepper and reserve. Spoon the stuffing into the cavity of the squid and secure the tops with cocktail sticks.

Place the squid in the cooking dish and sprinkle over 2 tablespoons each oil and water. Place in the slow cooker, cover with the lid. Switch to high and cook for 30 minutes. Mix together the remaining garlic, the tomatoes, chilli flakes, oregano and red pepper, then blend in a food processor and season to taste. Sprinkle over the stuffed squid and reduce the heat to low. Continue to cook for 1 hour. Serve with some assorted salad leaves.

Pea ❧ Prawn Risotto

Serves 6

450 g/1 lb whole raw prawns
125 g/4 oz butter
1 red onion, peeled and chopped
4 garlic cloves, peeled and finely chopped
225 g/8 oz easy-cook or Arborio rice
150 ml/¼ pint dry white wine
600 ml/1 pint vegetable or fish stock
375 g/13 oz frozen peas
4 tbsp freshly chopped mint
salt and freshly ground black pepper

Peel the prawns and reserve the heads and shells. Remove the black vein from the back of each prawn, then wash and dry on absorbent kitchen paper. Melt half the butter in a large frying pan, add the prawns' heads and shells and fry, stirring occasionally, for 3–4 minutes until golden. Strain the butter, discard the heads and shells and return the butter to the pan.

Add a further 25 g/1 oz of the butter to the pan and fry the onion and garlic for 5 minutes until softened but not coloured. Add the rice and stir the grains in the butter for 1 minute, then transfer to the cooking dish. Add the white wine and half the stock and switch to high. Cook for 30 minutes.

Stir the remaining stock into the rice, stir well, then re–cover and cook for 40 minutes. Stir once halfway through the cooking time.

Melt the remaining butter and stir-fry the prawns for 3–4 minutes. Stir into the rice, along with all the pan juices and the peas. Add the chopped mint and season to taste with salt and pepper. Reduce the temperature to low and leave for 10–15 minutes for all the flavours to infuse with one another before serving.

Cod Steaks with Saffron Aïoli

Serves 4

For the saffron aïoli

2 garlic cloves, peeled
1/4 tsp saffron strands
sea salt, to taste
1 medium egg yolk
200 ml/7 fl oz extra virgin
olive oil
2 tbsp lemon juice

For the marinade

2 tbsp olive oil
4 garlic cloves, peeled and finely chopped
1 red onion, peeled and chopped
1 tbsp freshly chopped rosemary
2 tbsp freshly chopped thyme
4–6 fresh rosemary sprigs
1 lemon, sliced
4 x 175 g/6 oz thick cod fillets
with skin
freshly cooked vegetables,
to serve

Crush the garlic, saffron and a pinch salt in a pestle and mortar to form a paste. Place in a blender with the egg yolk and blend for 30 seconds. With the motor running, slowly add the olive oil in a thin, steady stream until the mayonnaise is smooth and thick. Spoon into a small bowl and stir in the lemon juice. Cover and leave in the refrigerator until required.

Combine the olive oil, garlic, red onion, rosemary and thyme for the marinade and leave to infuse for about 10 minutes.

Place the sprigs of rosemary and slices of lemon in the base of the cooking dish and drizzle over a little more oil. Add the cod, skinned side up. Pour over the prepared marinade and cover with the lid.

Switch to high and cook for 30 minutes. Switch to auto and cook for 1 hour, or until the cod is cooked and the flesh opaque. Switch the slow cooker off and leave the cod to rest for 5 minutes before serving with the saffron aïoli and vegetables.

Garlic Baked Monkfish

Serves 4

300 g/10 oz parsnips, peeled
350 g/12 oz sweet potatoes, peeled
300 g/10 oz carrots, peeled
2 onions, peeled
4–6 garlic cloves, peeled
salt and freshly ground
black pepper
450 ml/³/4 pint fish or
vegetable stock
2 tbsp olive oil
2 small monkfish tails, about
900g/2 lb total weight, or
4 monkfish fillets, about
700 g/1¹/2 lb total weight
2–3 fresh rosemary sprigs
2 yellow peppers, deseeded
225 g/8 oz cherry tomatoes
2 tbsp freshly chopped parsley

Cut all the root vegetables, including the onions, into even-sized wedges and place in the cooking dish. Reserve 2 garlic cloves and add the remainder to the vegetables. Season to taste with salt and pepper and pour over 1 tablespoon of the oil. Turn the vegetables over until lightly coated in the oil. Pour in the stock, then cover with the lid and switch the cooker to auto. Cook for 4–5 hours.

Meanwhile, cut the monkfish tails into fillets. Using a sharp knife, cut down both sides of the central bone to form 2 fillets from each tail. Discard any skin or membrane, then rinse thoroughly. Make small incisions down the length of the monkfish fillets.

Cut the reserved garlic cloves into small slivers and break the rosemary into small sprigs. Insert the garlic and rosemary into the incisions in the fish. Cut the peppers into strips, then add to the vegetables together with the cherry tomatoes. Cook for a further 1 hour.

Place the fish on top and drizzle with the remaining oil. Cook for a further 1 hour, or reduce the heat to low and cook for 2 hours, or until the vegetables and fish are thoroughly cooked. Serve sprinkled with chopped parsley.

Mediterranean Fish Stew

Serves 4–6

4 tbsp olive oil
1 onion, peeled and
finely sliced
5 garlic cloves, peeled and finely sliced
1 fennel bulb, finely chopped
3 celery stalks, finely chopped
400 g can chopped tomatoes
with Italian herbs
1 tbsp freshly chopped oregano
1 bay leaf
zest and juice of 1 orange
1 tsp saffron strands
750 ml/1¼ pints fish stock
3 tbsp dry vermouth
salt and freshly ground
black pepper
225 g/8 oz thick haddock fillets
225 g/8 oz sea bass or
bream fillets
225 g/8 oz raw tiger
prawns, peeled
crusty bread, to serve

Heat the olive oil in a large saucepan. Add the onion, garlic, fennel and celery and cook over a low heat for 15 minutes, stirring frequently, until the vegetables are soft and just beginning to turn brown.

Add the canned tomatoes with their juice, the oregano, bay leaf, orange zest and juice and the saffron strands. Bring to the boil, then reduce the heat and simmer for 5 minutes. Add the fish stock and vermouth and season to taste with salt and pepper, then pour into the cooking dish. Cover with the lid and switch to high and cook for 1 hour.

Wipe or rinse the haddock and bass fillets and remove as many of the bones as possible. Place on a chopping board and cut into 5 cm/2 inch cubes. Add to the cooking dish and switch to auto. Cook for 30 minutes before adding the prawns and continue to cook for a further 20 minutes, or until the prawns are cooked and have turned pink. Adjust the seasoning to taste and serve with crusty bread.

Salmon with Herb Risotto

Serves 4

4 x 175 g/6 oz salmon fillets
3–4 tbsp plain flour
1 tsp dried mustard powder
salt and freshly ground
black pepper
2 tbsp olive oil
3 shallots, peeled and chopped
225 g/8 oz easy-cook or
Arborio rice
150 ml/¼ pint dry white wine
600 ml/1 pint vegetable or
fish stock
50 g/2 oz butter
2 tbsp freshly snipped chives
2 tbsp freshly chopped dill
2 tbsp freshly chopped parsley

To garnish
lemon slices
fresh dill sprigs
tomato salad, to serve

Wipe the salmon fillets with a clean, damp cloth. Mix together the flour, mustard powder and seasoning on a large plate and use to coat the salmon fillets and reserve.

Heat half the olive oil in a large frying pan and fry the shallots for 5 minutes until softened but not coloured. Add the rice and stir for 1 minute, then slowly add the wine and bring to the boil. Slowly pour in the stock, then return to the boil.

Carefully transfer to the cooking dish and pour in the remaining stock. Cover with the lid and cook on high for 40 minutes, stirring once during cooking.

Stir in the butter and freshly chopped herbs and season to taste with salt and pepper. Place the salmon on top of the rice and continue to cook for 40–60 minutes until the salmon is cooked. Serve garnished with slices of lemon and sprigs of dill and serve immediately with the tomato salad.

Bouillabaisse

Serves 4

700 g/1¹/₂ lb assorted fish, e.g. whiting, mackerel, red mullet, salmon and king prawns, cleaned and skinned
few saffron strands
3 tbsp olive oil
2 onions, peeled and sliced
2 celery stalks, trimmed and sliced
225 g/8 oz ripe tomatoes, peeled and chopped
1 fresh bay leaf
2–3 garlic cloves, peeled and crushed
1 bouquet garni
sea salt and freshly ground black pepper
french bread to serve

Cut the fish into thick pieces, peel the prawns if necessary, and rinse well. Place the saffron strands in a small bowl, cover with warm water and leave to infuse for at least 10 minutes.

Heat the oil in a large, heavy-based saucepan or casserole dish, add the onions and celery and sauté for 5 minutes, stirring occasionally. Add the tomatoes, bay leaf, garlic and bouquet garni and stir until lightly coated with the oil.

Transfer to the cooking dish and place the firm fish on the base. Pour in the saffron-infused water and enough water to just cover. Cover with the lid and switch to high. Cook for 1 hour.

Add the soft-flesh fish and switch the slow cooker to auto and cook for 2 hours, or reduce the cooker to low and cook for 4 hours. Season to taste with salt and pepper, remove and discard the bouquet garni and serve with French bread.

Meat

Dishes

Meat dishes are a great way to feed a hungry family, but are sometimes very time consuming. A slow cooker will allow you to make fantastic hearty meals, such as Spaghetti Bolognese, which cooks to perfection in a slow cooker and lets all those flavours really come to life. For something new, try your hand at Spicy Lamb in Yogurt Sauce or delicious Chinese style Hoisin Pork!

Lamb Pilaf

Serves 4

2 tbsp vegetable oil
25 g/1 oz flaked almonds
1 medium onion, peeled and
finely chopped
1 medium carrot, peeled and
finely chopped
1 celery stalk, finely chopped
350 g/12 oz small pieces lamb
1/4 tsp ground cinnamon
1/4 tsp chilli flakes
2 large tomatoes, skinned, deseeded
and chopped
grated zest of 1 orange
300 g/11 oz easy-cook basmati rice
750 ml/1 1/4 pints vegetable or lamb stock
2 tbsp freshly snipped chives
3 tbsp freshly chopped coriander
salt and freshly ground black pepper

To garnish
lemon slices
fresh coriander sprigs

Heat the oil in a flameproof casserole dish with a tight-fitting lid
and add the almonds. Cook for about 1 minute until just starting to
brown, stirring often. Add the onion, carrot and celery and cook
gently for a further 8–10 minutes until soft and lightly browned.

Increase the heat and add the lamb. Cook for a further 5 minutes
until the lamb has changed colour. Add the ground cinnamon and
chilli flakes and stir briefly before adding the tomatoes and
orange zest.

Stir and add the rice, then the stock. Transfer to the cooking dish
and cover with the lid. Switch the slow cooker to high and cook for
1 1/2–2 hours until the rice is tender and the stock is absorbed.

Switch the cooker off and leave to stand for 5 minutes before
stirring in the chives and coriander. Season to taste with salt and
pepper. Garnish with the lemon slices and sprigs of fresh
coriander and serve immediately.

Slow-cooked Lamb

ℰ

Serves 4

1 leg of lamb, about 1.4 kg/
3 lb in weight
2 tbsp vegetable oil
1 tsp fennel seeds
1 tsp cumin seeds
1 tsp ground coriander
1 tsp turmeric
2 garlic cloves, peeled
and crushed
2 green chillies, deseeded
and chopped
freshly cooked vegetables,
to serve

For the potatoes

550 g/1¼ lb potatoes, peeled
2 onions, peeled
4 garlic cloves, peeled

Wipe the lamb with absorbent kitchen paper and make small slits over the meat. Reserve.

Heat the oil in a frying pan, add the seeds and fry for 30 seconds, stirring. Add the remaining spices, including the 2 garlic cloves and green chillies, and cook for 5 minutes. Remove and use half to spread over the lamb.

Cut the potatoes into bite-size chunks and the onions into wedges. Cut the garlic in half. Place in the cooking dish and cover with the remaining spice paste, then place the lamb on top.

Cover with the lid and switch the slow cooker to auto for 1 hour. Switch the cooker to low and continue to cook for 6–8 hours until the lamb and potatoes are cooked. Serve the lamb with the potatoes and freshly cooked vegetables.

Lamb 🕸 Potato Curry

Serves 4

450 g/1 lb lean lamb, such
as leg steaks
2 tbsp vegetable oil
2 onions, peeled and cut
into wedges
2–3 garlic cloves, peeled
and sliced
2 celery stalks, trimmed and sliced
5 cm/2 inch piece fresh root ginger, peeled
and grated
2 green chillies, deseeded
and chopped
few curry leaves
1 tsp ground cumin
1 tsp ground coriander
1 tsp turmeric
1 tbsp tomato purée
150 ml/$\frac{1}{4}$ pint water
150 ml/$\frac{1}{4}$ pint coconut milk
225 g/8 oz tomatoes, chopped
450 g/1 lb new potatoes, scrubbed
125 g/4 oz carrots, peeled
and sliced

Discard any fat or gristle from the lamb, then cut into thin strips and reserve.

Heat the oil in a deep frying pan, add the onions, garlic and celery and fry for 5 minutes, or until softened. Add the ginger, chillies, curry leaves and spices and continue to fry for a further 3 minutes, stirring constantly. Add the lamb and cook for 5 minutes, or until coated in the spices.

Blend the tomato purée with the water, then stir into the pan together with the coconut milk and chopped tomatoes.

Cut the potatoes into small chunks and add to the pan with the carrots. Bring to the boil, then transfer to the cooking dish. Switch the slow cooker to low and cook for 6–8 hours. Serve.

Braised Lamb with Broad Beans

Serves 4

700 g/1½ lb lean lamb, cut
into large chunks
1 tbsp plain flour
1 onion
2 garlic cloves
1 tbsp olive oil
400 g can chopped tomatoes with basil
300 ml/½ pint lamb stock
2 tsp dried thyme
2 tsp dried oregano
salt and freshly ground
black pepper
150 g/5 oz frozen broad beans, thawed
fresh oregano, to garnish
creamy mashed potatoes,
to serve

Trim the lamb, discarding any fat or gristle, then place the flour in a polythene bag, add the lamb and toss until coated thoroughly. Peel and slice the onion and garlic and reserve.

Heat the olive oil in a heavy-based saucepan and, when hot, add the lamb and cook, stirring, until the meat is sealed and browned all over. Using a slotted spoon, remove and reserve.

Add the onion and garlic to the saucepan and cook for 3 minutes, stirring frequently, until softened, then return the lamb to the saucepan. Add the chopped tomatoes with their juice, the stock, the chopped thyme and oregano to the pan and season to taste with salt and pepper. Bring to the boil, then transfer to the cooking dish. Cover with the lid and switch to low. Cook for 4–6 hours.

Add the broad beans to the lamb and continue to cook on low for 2 hours, or until the lamb is tender. Garnish with fresh oregano and serve with creamy mashed potatoes.

Lamb Balti

Serves 4–6

450 g/1 lb lean lamb, such as fillet, trimmed
2 tbsp vegetable oil or ghee
1 tsp mustard seeds
1 tsp ground coriander
1 tsp ground cumin
$^1/_2$ tsp turmeric
$^1/_2$ tsp asafoetida
1 tsp garam masala
2–3 garlic cloves, peeled
and crushed
2–3 green chillies, deseeded
and chopped
2 onions, peeled and chopped
1 aubergine, trimmed and chopped
4 tomatoes, chopped
2 tsp tomato purée
600 ml/1 pint lamb or
vegetable stock
2 tbsp freshly chopped coriander
naan bread, to serve

Dice the lamb and reserve. Heat the oil or ghee in a large frying pan, add the mustard seeds and fry for 30 seconds, or until they pop.

Add the remaining spices and cook for 2 minutes, stirring, before adding the garlic, chillies, onions and aubergine. Cook, stirring, for a further 5 minutes, or until the vegetables are coated in the spices.

Add the lamb and continue to fry for 5–8 minutes until sealed. Stir in the chopped tomatoes. Blend the tomato purée with the stock, then pour into the pan. Bring to the boil, then transfer to the cooking dish. Cover with the lid and switch to low. Cook for 6–8 hours until the lamb is tender. Sprinkle with chopped coriander and serve with plenty of naan bread.

Lamb Passanda

Serves 4

550 g/1¼ lb lean lamb
2 tbsp vegetable oil or ghee
1 tsp ground cumin
1 tsp ground coriander
1 tsp turmeric
½ tsp fenugreek seeds
3 green cardamom pods, cracked
1 cinnamon stick, bruised
3 whole cloves
5 cm/2 inch piece root ginger, grated
1–2 green chillies, deseeded and finely chopped
2–4 garlic cloves, crushed
2 red onions, peeled and chopped
150 ml/¼ pint natural yogurt
85 ml/3 fl oz coconut cream
1 green pepper, deseeded and sliced
50 g/2 oz sultanas
3 tbsp ground almonds
25 g/1 oz blanched almonds
25 g/1 oz unsalted cashews, chopped

Discard any fat or gristle from the lamb, cut into thin strips and reserve. Heat the oil or ghee in a large frying pan, add the spices, including the cinnamon and cloves, and cook for 3 minutes.

Add the ginger, chillies, garlic, onions and meat and cook, stirring, until the meat is coated in the spices.

Stir in the yogurt, then spoon into a bowl, cover and leave to marinate in the refrigerator for 15 minutes.

Place the meat mixture into the cooking dish and cover with the lid. Switch the slow cooker to auto and cook for 1 hour.

Pour in the coconut cream and add the green pepper and sultanas. Stir in the ground almonds. Cook on auto for a further 30 minutes, then switch to low and cook for a further 5 hours. Spoon into a warmed serving dish, sprinkle with the nuts and serve.

Lamb Meatballs

ℰ

450 g/1 lb fresh lamb mince
1 tbsp freshly chopped parsley
1 tbsp freshly grated root ginger
1 tbsp light soy sauce
1 medium egg yolk
4 tbsp dark soy sauce
2 tbsp dry sherry
150 ml/¼ pint lamb or
vegetable stock
1½ tbsp cornflour
1 tbsp vegetable oil
2 garlic cloves, peeled
and chopped
1 bunch spring onions, trimmed and
shredded
½ Savoy cabbage, trimmed
and shredded
½ head Chinese leaves, trimmed
and shredded
freshly chopped red chilli,
to garnish

Place the lamb mince in a large bowl with the parsley, ginger, light soy sauce and egg yolk and mix together. Divide the mixture into walnut-size pieces and, using your hands, roll into balls. Place on a large plate or baking sheet, cover with clingfilm and chill in the refrigerator for at least 30 minutes.

Meanwhile, blend together the dark soy sauce, sherry, stock and cornflour with 2 tablespoons water in a small bowl until smooth. Reserve.

Lightly brush the cooking dish with the vegetable oil and add the meatballs. Add the garlic and spring onions. Cover with the lid and switch the slow cooker to high. Cook for 30 minutes, then turn the meatballs over.

Cover the Savoy cabbage and the Chinese leaves with boiling water and leave for 1 minute, drain, then add to the cooking dish and pour over the reserved soy sauce mixture. Continue to cook for 1 hour. Garnish with the chopped red chilli and serve immediately.

Sausage 🍂 Apple Pot

Serves 4

1 tbsp olive oil
1 onion, peeled and sliced
2–3 garlic cloves, peeled
and sliced
2 celery stalks, trimmed
and sliced
8 apple and pork
large sausages
300 g/11 oz carrots,
peeled and sliced
1 large cooking apple,
peeled and sliced
300 g/11 oz courgettes,
trimmed and sliced
salt and freshly ground
black pepper
600 ml/1 pint vegetable stock
2 tsp dried mixed herbs
450 g/1 lb potatoes, peeled
and grated
50 g/2 oz Gruyère cheese, grated

Heat the oil in a frying pan, add the onion, garlic and celery and fry for 5 minutes. Push the vegetables to one side, then add the sausages and cook, turning the sausages over, until browned.

Spoon all the fried ingredients into the cooking dish. Arrange the onions over and around the sausages together with the carrots, apple and courgettes. Season to taste with salt and pepper and pour over the stock. Sprinkle with the mixed herbs, cover with the lid and switch the slow cooker to high, then cook for 1 hour. Switch the cooker to auto and cook for 3–5 hours.

Meanwhile, soak the grated potatoes in a bowl of cold water for 10 minutes. Drain thoroughly, then place the potatoes on a clean tea towel and squeeze to remove any excess moisture. Remove the lid from the slow cooker and place the grated potatoes on top. Sprinkle with the grated cheese and re-cover with the lid. Cook for a further 1–2 hours. If liked, just before serving, remove the lid and place the dish under a preheated grill. Cook for 5–10 minutes until the topping is crisp, turning the dish around to ensure that all the topping becomes crisp.

Cassoulet Surprise

č

Serves 4

1 tbsp olive oil

1 onion, peeled and chopped

2 celery stalks, trimmed
and chopped

175 g/6 oz carrots, peeled
and sliced

2–3 garlic cloves, peeled
and crushed

350 g/12 oz pork belly

8 spicy thick sausages, such
as Toulouse

few fresh thyme sprigs

salt and freshly ground
black pepper

2 x 400 g/14 oz cans cannellini beans,
drained and rinsed

600 ml/1 pint vegetable stock

75 g/3 oz fresh breadcrumbs

2 tbsp freshly chopped thyme

Heat the oil in a large saucepan or frying pan, add the onion, celery, carrots and garlic and fry for 5 minutes. Cut the pork into small pieces and cut the sausages into chunks.

Add the meat to the vegetables and cook for 5 minutes, stirring, until lightly browned.

Add the thyme sprigs and season to taste with salt and pepper, then spoon all the fried ingredients into the cooking dish. Spoon the beans on top, then pour in the stock.

Mix the breadcrumbs with 1 tablespoon of the chopped thyme in a small bowl and sprinkle on top of the beans. Cover with the lid and switch the slow cooker to high for 1 hour, then switch to low and cook for 6–8 hours. Remove the lid and either place under a preheated grill and cook for 5–10 minutes, turning the dish occasionally until the breadcrumbs are crisp, or serve immediately sprinkled with the remaining chopped thyme.

Leek ❧ Ham Risotto

Serves 4

1 tbsp olive oil
25 g/1 oz butter
1 medium onion, peeled and
finely chopped
4 leeks, trimmed and
thinly sliced
1½ tbsp freshly chopped thyme
300 g/11 oz Arborio rice
750 ml/1¼ pints vegetable or
chicken stock, heated
225 g/8 oz cooked ham
175 g/6 oz peas, thawed if frozen
50 g/2 oz Parmesan
cheese, grated
salt and freshly ground
black pepper

Heat the oil and half the butter together in a large saucepan. Add the onion and leeks and cook over a medium heat for 6–8 minutes, stirring occasionally, until soft and beginning to colour. Stir in the thyme and cook briefly.

Add the rice and stir well. Continue stirring over a medium heat for about 1 minute until the rice is glossy. Stir in the stock and carefully transfer to the cooking dish. Cover with the lid, then switch to high and cook for 30 minutes.

Meanwhile, either chop or finely shred the ham, then add to the rice together with the peas. Continue to cook on low for 1 hour, or until the rice is tender and the ham is piping hot.

Switch the cooker off and add the remaining butter; sprinkle over the Parmesan cheese and season to taste with salt and pepper. When the butter has melted and the cheese has softened, stir well to blend the flavours together. Taste and adjust the seasoning if necessary, then serve immediately.

Risi e Bisi

Serves 4

700 g/1½ lb young peas in pods,
or 175 g/6 oz frozen petits pois
25 g/1 oz unsalted butter
1 tsp olive oil
3 rashers pancetta, chopped
1 small onion, peeled and
finely chopped
1 garlic clove, peeled and
finely chopped
600 ml/1 pint vegetable stock
pinch caster sugar
1 tsp lemon juice
1 bay leaf
200 g/7 oz Arborio rice
3 tbsp freshly chopped parsley
50 g/2 oz Parmesan cheese,
finely grated
salt and freshly ground
black pepper

To garnish
fresh parsley sprigs
julienne strips orange zest

Shell the peas, if using fresh ones. Melt the butter and olive oil together in a large, heavy-based saucepan. Add the chopped pancetta, the chopped onion and garlic and gently fry for about 10 minutes until the onion is softened and is just beginning to colour.

Add the caster sugar, lemon juice and bay leaf, then pour in the vegetable stock. Add the fresh peas, if using. Bring the mixture to a fast boil. Add the rice and carefully transfer to the cooking dish and cover with the lid. Switch the slow cooker to high and cook for 1 hour, or until the rice is tender. If using thawed frozen petits pois, add to the rice and continue to cook for 30 minutes.

When the rice is cooked, remove the bay leaf and discard. Stir in 2½ tablespoons of the chopped parsley and the grated Parmesan cheese. Season to taste with salt and pepper. Transfer the rice to a large serving dish. Garnish with the remaining chopped parsley, a sprig of fresh parsley and julienne strips of orange zest. Serve immediately while piping hot.

Hoisin Pork

⚔

Serves 4

1.4 kg/3 lb piece lean belly pork, boned
sea salt
2 tsp Chinese five-spice powder
2 garlic cloves, peeled
and chopped
2 tsp sesame oil
4 tbsp hoisin sauce
1 tbsp clear honey
150 ml/¼ pint pork stock
assorted salad leaves,
to garnish

Using a sharp knife, cut the pork skin in a crisscross pattern, making sure not to cut all the way through into the flesh. Rub the salt evenly over the skin and leave to stand for 30 minutes.

Meanwhile, mix together the five-spice powder, garlic, one teaspoon of the sesame oil, hoisin sauce and honey until smooth. Rub the mixture evenly over the pork skin. Place the pork on a plate and chill in the refrigerator to marinate for up to 6 hours.

Lightly brush the cooking dish with the remaining sesame oil, then place the pork in the dish. Pour over the stock and cover with the lid. Switch the slow cooker to auto and cook for 1 hour. Turn the cooker to low and continue to cook for 5–7 hours until the juices run clear when pierced with a skewer.

Switch the slow cooker off and leave the pork to rest for 10 minutes, then cut into strips. Arrange on a warmed serving platter. Garnish with salad leaves and serve immediately.

Lamb ❧ Date Tagine

Serves 4

few saffron strands
1 tbsp olive oil
1 onion, peeled and cut
into wedges
2–3 garlic cloves, peeled
and sliced
550 g/1¼ lb lean lamb, such as
neck fillet, diced
1 cinnamon stick, bruised
1 tsp ground cumin
225 g/8 oz carrots, peeled
and sliced
350 g/12 oz sweet potato, peeled
and diced
900 ml/1½ pints lamb or
vegetable stock
salt and freshly ground
black pepper
125 g/4 oz dates (fresh or dried),
pitted and halved
freshly prepared couscous,
to serve

Place the saffron in a small bowl, cover with warm water and leave to infuse for 10 minutes. Heat the oil in a large, heavy-based pan, add the onion, garlic and lamb and fry for 8–10 minutes until sealed. Add the cinnamon stick and ground cumin and cook, stirring constantly, for a further 2 minutes.

Add the carrots and sweet potato, then add the saffron with the soaking liquid and the stock. Bring to the boil, then season to taste with salt and pepper. Carefully transfer to the cooking dish and cover with the lid. Switch the slow cooker to high and cook for 1 hour, then switch to low and continue to cook for 4–6 hours.

Add the dates and continue to cook for a further hour. Remove the cinnamon stick, adjust the seasoning and serve with freshly prepared couscous.

Pork Cabbage Parcels

Serves 4

8 large green cabbage leaves
1 tbsp vegetable oil
2 celery stalks, trimmed
and chopped
1 carrot, peeled and cut
into matchsticks
125 g/4 oz fresh pork mince
50 g/2 oz button mushrooms,
wiped and sliced
1 tsp Chinese five-spice powder
50 g/2 oz cooked long-grain rice
juice of 1 lemon
1 tbsp soy sauce
150 ml/¼ pint chicken stock

For the tomato sauce

1 tbsp vegetable oil
1 bunch spring onions, trimmed
and chopped
400 g can chopped tomatoes
1 tbsp light soy sauce
1 tbsp freshly chopped mint
freshly ground black pepper

To make the tomato sauce, heat the oil in a heavy-based saucepan, add the spring onions and cook for 2 minutes, or until softened.

Add the tomatoes, soy sauce and mint to the saucepan, bring to the boil, cover, then simmer for 10 minutes. Season to taste with pepper. Reheat when required.

Meanwhile, blanch the cabbage leaves in a large saucepan of lightly salted water for 3 minutes. Drain and refresh under cold running water. Pat dry with absorbent kitchen paper and reserve.

Heat the oil in a small saucepan, add the celery, carrot and pork mince and cook for 3 minutes. Add the mushrooms and cook for 3 minutes. Stir in the Chinese five-spice powder, rice, lemon juice and soy sauce and mix together.

Place some of the filling in the centre of each cabbage leaf and fold to enclose the filling. Place in the cooking dish seam side down. Pour over the stock and cover with the lid. Switch the slow cooker to auto and cook for 2–4 hours. Serve immediately with the reheated tomato sauce.

Spaghetti Bolognese

Serves 4

1 carrot
2 celery stalks
1 onion
2 garlic cloves
450 g/1 lb lean
minced beef
225 g/8 oz smoked streaky
bacon, chopped
1 tbsp plain flour
150 ml/¼ pint red wine
400 g can chopped tomatoes
2 tbsp tomato purée
2 tsp dried mixed herbs
salt and freshly ground
black pepper
pinch sugar
350 g/12 oz spaghetti
fresh oregano sprigs, to garnish
Parmesan cheese shavings,
to serve

Peel and chop the carrot, trim and chop the celery, then peel and chop the onion and garlic.

Heat a large, nonstick frying pan and fry the beef and bacon for 5–10 minutes, stirring occasionally, until browned. Add the prepared vegetables to the frying pan and cook for about 3 minutes until softened, stirring occasionally.

Add the flour and cook for 1 minute. Stir in the red wine, tomatoes, tomato purée, mixed herbs, seasoning to taste and sugar. Carefully transfer to the cooking dish and cover with the lid. Switch the slow cooker to auto and cook for 6–8 hours.

Just before serving, bring a large saucepan of lightly salted water to the boil and cook the spaghetti for 10–12 minutes until *al dente*. Drain well and divide between four serving plates. Spoon over the sauce, garnish with a few sprigs of oregano and serve immediately with plenty of Parmesan shavings.

Italian Beef 'Pot Roast'

Serves 6

1.8 kg/4 lb brisket of beef
225 g/8 oz small onions, peeled
3 garlic cloves, peeled
and chopped
2 celery stalks, trimmed
and chopped
2 carrots, peeled and sliced
450 g/1 lb ripe tomatoes
300 ml/$\frac{1}{2}$ pint Italian red wine
2 tbsp olive oil
300 ml/$\frac{1}{2}$ pint beef stock
1 tbsp tomato purée
2 tsp freeze-dried
mixed herbs
salt and freshly ground
black pepper
25 g/1 oz butter
25 g/1 oz plain flour
freshly cooked vegetables,
to serve

Place the beef in a bowl. Add the onions, garlic, celery and carrots. Place the tomatoes in a separate small bowl and cover with boiling water. Stand for 2 minutes and drain. Peel away the skins, discard the seeds and chop, then add to the bowl with the red wine. Cover tightly and marinate in the refrigerator overnight.

Lift the marinated beef from the bowl and pat dry with kitchen paper. Heat the olive oil in a frying pan and cook the beef until it is browned all over, then remove and place in the cooking dish. Drain the vegetables, reserving the marinade. Add the vegetables to the frying pan and fry gently for 5 minutes, stirring occasionally, until all the vegetables are browned. Place in the cooking dish.

Blend the marinade, beef stock, tomato purée, mixed herbs and seasoning together. Bring to the boil, then pour over the beef and cover with the lid. Switch the slow cooker to auto and cook for 3 hours, then switch to low and cook for 8–10 hours.

Using a slotted spoon, transfer the beef and any large vegetables to a plate and leave in a warm place. Blend the butter and flour into a paste. Pour the meat juices into a small saucepan and bring to the boil. Stir in small spoonfuls of the butter and flour paste to thicken. Serve with the sauce and cooked vegetables.

Beef Bourguignon

č

Serves 4

700 g/1½ lb braising
steak, trimmed
225 g/8 oz piece pork belly
or lardons
2 tbsp olive oil
12 shallots, peeled
2 garlic cloves, peeled
and sliced
225 g/8 oz carrots, peeled
and sliced
2 tbsp plain flour
3 tbsp brandy (optional)
150 ml/¼ pint red wine, such
as a Burgundy
450 ml/¾ pint beef stock
1 bay leaf
salt and freshly ground
black pepper
450 g/1 lb new potatoes, scrubbed
1 tbsp freshly chopped parsley,
to garnish

Cut the steak and pork into small pieces and reserve. Heat 1 tablespoon of the oil in a frying pan, add the meat and cook in batches for 5–8 minutes until sealed. Remove with a slotted spoon and reserve.

Add the remaining oil to the pan, then add the shallots, carrots and garlic and cook for 10 minutes. Return the meat to the shallots and sprinkle in the flour. Cook for 2 minutes, stirring occasionally, before pouring in the brandy, if using. Heat for 1 minute, then take off the heat and ignite.

When the flames have subsided, pour in the wine and stock. Return to the heat and bring to the boil, stirring constantly.

Transfer to the cooking dish. Cut the potatoes in half and stir into the meat. Add the bay leaf and season to taste with salt and pepper. Cover with the lid and switch the slow cooker to high. Cook for 2 hours.

Turn the slow cooker to low and continue to cook for 8–10 hours until the meat and potatoes are tender. Serve sprinkled with chopped parsley.

Meatballs with Olives

ℰ

Serves 4

250 g/9 oz shallots, peeled
2–3 garlic cloves, peeled
450 g/1 lb fresh beef mince
2 tbsp fresh white or wholemeal
breadcrumbs
3 tbsp freshly chopped basil
salt and freshly ground
black pepper
2 tbsp olive oil
5 tbsp ready-made
pesto sauce
5 tbsp mascarpone cheese
50 g/2 oz pitted black
olives, halved
275 g/10 oz thick pasta noodles
freshly chopped flat-leaf parsley
fresh flat-leaf parsley sprigs, to garnish
freshly grated Parmesan
cheese, to serve

Finely chop two of the shallots and place in a bowl with the garlic, beef, breadcrumbs, basil and seasoning to taste. With damp hands, bring the mixture together and shape into small balls about the size of an apricot.

Heat the olive oil in a frying pan and cook the meatballs for 3–4 minutes, turning occasionally, until browned. Remove and drain on absorbent kitchen paper. Place in the cooking dish. Slice the remaining shallots, add to the pan and cook for 5 minutes until softened. Blend the pesto and mascarpone together, then stir into the pan with the olives.

Bring to the boil, then pour over the meatballs and cover with the lid. Switch the slow cooker to auto and cook for 1 hour. Turn the cooker to low and cook for 3–4 hours.

Just before serving, bring a large saucepan of lightly salted water to the boil and cook the noodles for 8–10 minutes until *al dente*. Drain the noodles, reserving 2 tablespoons of the cooking liquor. Return the noodles to the pan with the reserved cooking liquor. Stir the noodles and heat for 2 minutes.

Serve the noodles topped with the meatballs and their sauce. Sprinkle with chopped parsley. Garnish with a few sprigs of parsley and serve immediately with grated Parmesan cheese.

Steak & Kidney Stew

Serves 4

1 tbsp olive oil
1 onion, peeled and chopped
2–3 garlic cloves, crushed
2 celery stalks, sliced
550 g/1¹/4 lb diced braising steak
125 g/4 oz lambs' kidneys, cored and chopped
2 tbsp plain flour
1 tbsp tomato purée
900 ml/1¹/2 pints beef stock
salt and freshly ground black pepper
1 fresh bay leaf
300 g/11 oz carrots, peeled and sliced
350 g/12 oz baby new potatoes, scrubbed
350 g/12 oz spinach leaves, chopped

For the dumplings

125 g/4 oz self-raising flour
50 g/2 oz shredded suet
1 tbsp freshly chopped mixed herbs
2–3 tbsp water

Heat the oil in a large, heavy-based saucepan, add the onion, garlic and celery and sauté for 5 minutes, or until browned. Remove from the pan with a slotted spoon and reserve. Add the steak and kidneys to the pan and cook for 3–5 minutes until sealed, then return the onion mixture to the pan. Sprinkle in the flour and cook, stirring, for 2 minutes. Take off the heat, stir in the tomato purée, then the stock, and season to taste with salt and pepper. Add the bay leaf.

Return to the heat and bring to the boil, stirring occasionally. Add the carrots and potatoes, then carefully transfer to the cooking dish. Cover with the lid and switch the slow cooker to high. Cook for 1 hour, then switch to low and cook for 6–8 hours.

Place the flour, suet and herbs in a bowl and add a little seasoning. Add the water and mix to a stiff mixture. Using a little extra flour, shape into 8 small balls. Place the dumplings on top of the stew and cover with the lid. Return the slow cooker to high and cook for 30–60 minutes. Switch the cooker off and stir in the spinach. Leave to stand for 2 minutes, or until the spinach is wilted.

Massaman Beef Curry

Serves 4–6

450 g/1 lb braising steak
2 tbsp vegetable oil
5 cm/2 inch piece fresh root ginger,
peeled and grated
3 green bird's-eye chillies,
deseeded and chopped
2 red onions, peeled and chopped
3 garlic cloves, peeled
and crushed
2 tbsp Massaman Thai
curry paste
400 ml/14 fl oz coconut milk
150–200 ml/5–7 fl oz beef stock
350 g/12 oz new potatoes,
scrubbed and cut into
small chunks
1 green pepper, deseeded
and cut into strips
50 g/2 oz roasted peanuts,
chopped

Trim the beef, cut into thin strips and reserve. Heat the oil in a heavy-based frying pan, add the ginger and chillies and fry for 3 minutes. Add the onions and garlic and continue to fry for 5 minutes, or until the onions have softened.

Remove the onions and garlic with a slotted spoon and add the beef to the pan. Cook, stirring, for 5 minutes, or until sealed.

Add the curry paste and continue to fry for 3 minutes, then return the onions and garlic to the pan and stir well.

Pour the coconut milk and stock into the pan and add the new potatoes, then bring to the boil. Transfer to the cooking dish and cover with the lid. Switch the slow cooker to auto and cook for 2 hours.

Add the green pepper to the meat and switch the slow cooker to low. Cook for 6–8 hours until the meat and potatoes are cooked. Sprinkle the chopped peanuts over the cooked curry and serve.

Kerala Pork Curry

Serves 4–6

450 g/1 lb pork loin, trimmed
2 tbsp vegetable oil or ghee
1 tbsp desiccated coconut
1 tsp mustard seeds
1 tsp fennel seeds
1 cinnamon stick, bruised
1 tsp ground cumin
1 tsp ground coriander
1–2 red chillies, deseeded and chopped
2–3 garlic cloves, peeled and chopped
2 onions, peeled and chopped
$^1/_2$ tsp saffron strands
300 ml/$^1/_2$ pint coconut milk
150 ml/$^1/_4$ pint water
125 g/4 oz frozen peas, thawed
freshly cooked basmati rice, to serve

Cut the pork into small chunks and reserve. Heat 1 teaspoon of the oil or ghee in a frying pan, add the desiccated coconut and fry for 30 seconds, stirring, until lightly toasted. Reserve.

Add the remaining oil or ghee to the pan, add the seeds and fry for 30 seconds, or until they pop. Add the remaining spices and cook, stirring, for 2 minutes. Add the pork and fry for 5 minutes, or until sealed.

Add the chillies, garlic and onions and continue to fry for 3 minutes before stirring in the saffron strands. Stir, then pour in the coconut milk and water.

Transfer to the cooking dish and cover with the lid. Switch the slow cooker to auto and cook for 1 hour before switching the cooker to low and cooking for 5–7 hours. Stir the peas into the cooking dish for the last 1 hour of cooking time. Serve with freshly cooked basmati rice.

Braised Rabbit with Peppers

Serves 4

1.1 kg/2½ lb rabbit pieces
5 tbsp olive oil
finely grated zest and juice
of 1 lemon
2–3 tbsp freshly chopped thyme
salt and freshly ground
black pepper
1 onion, peeled and
thinly sliced
4 red peppers, deseeded
and cut into 2.5 cm/
1 inch pieces
2 garlic cloves, peeled
and crushed
400 g can tomatoes,
strained and pulped
1 tsp brown sugar
freshly cooked creamy mashed
potatoes, to serve

Place the rabbit pieces in a shallow dish with 2 tablespoons of the olive oil, the lemon zest and juice, thyme and black pepper. Turn until well coated, then cover and leave in the refrigerator to marinate for at least 1 hour.

Heat 2 tablespoons of the oil in a large frying pan, drain the rabbit, reserving the marinade, and pat the rabbit dry with absorbent kitchen paper. Add the rabbit to the pan and cook on all sides until golden, then remove and reserve.

Clean the frying pan and heat the remaining 1 tablespoon of the oil. Add the onion and cook gently for 5 minutes, then add the peppers and cook for a further 5 minutes, stirring occasionally. Stir in the garlic, crushed tomatoes and brown sugar and cook for 3 minutes.

Add the reserved marinade to the onion and tomato mixture and bring to the boil. Pour into the cooking dish and add the rabbit, making sure the rabbit is covered in the sauce, and cover with the lid.

Switch the slow cooker to high and cook for 1 hour. Switch to auto and cook for 3–4 hours. Serve the rabbit and the vegetable mixture on a bed of creamy mashed potatoes.

Spicy Lamb in Yogurt Sauce

Serves 4

1 tsp hot chilli powder
1 tsp ground cinnamon
1 tsp medium-hot curry powder
1 tsp ground cumin
salt and freshly ground black pepper
4 tbsp groundnut oil
450 g/1 lb lamb fillet, trimmed
4 cardamom pods, bruised
4 whole cloves
1 onion, peeled and
finely sliced
2 garlic cloves, peeled
and crushed
2.5 cm/1 inch piece fresh root
ginger, peeled and grated
150 ml/¼ pint Greek-style yogurt
1 tbsp freshly chopped coriander
2 spring onions, trimmed and
finely sliced

To serve
freshly cooked rice
naan bread

Blend the chilli powder, cinnamon, curry powder, cumin and seasoning with 2 tablespoons of the oil in a bowl and reserve.

Cut the lamb fillet into thin strips, add to the spice and oil mixture and stir until coated thoroughly. Cover and leave to marinate in the refrigerator for at least 30 minutes.

Heat a wok, then pour in the remaining oil. When hot, add the cardamom pods and cloves and stir-fry for 10 seconds. Add the onion, garlic and ginger to the wok and stir-fry for 3–4 minutes until softened.

Place the lamb with the marinade into the cooking dish and cover with the lid. Switch the cooker to auto and cook for 1 hour. Reduce the heat to low. Pour in the yogurt, stir thoroughly and cook for 4–5 hours. Sprinkle with the chopped coriander and sliced spring onions, then serve immediately with freshly cooked rice and naan bread.

Poultry

&

Game

Poultry and game are great staples and form the basis of a huge number of dishes. Chilli Baked Chicken is a great twist on a Sunday lunch, while Creamy Chicken and Rice Pilaf is a succulent dish sure to impress any hungry dinner party guest! Of course, there are also ample options for simple weekday suppers, such as the delicious Lemon Chicken Rice or Chicken with Porcini and Cream.

Chicken Basquaise

Serves 4–6

1.4 kg/3 lb chicken, cut
into 8 portions
2 tbsp plain flour
salt and freshly ground
black pepper
3 tbsp olive oil
1 large onion, peeled
and sliced
2 red peppers, deseeded and cut
into thick strips
2 garlic cloves, peeled and crushed
150 g/5 oz chorizo sausage, cut
into 1 cm/$\frac{1}{2}$ inch pieces
200 g/7 oz easy-cook white long-
grain rice
600 ml/1 pint chicken stock
1 tsp crushed dried chillies
$\frac{1}{2}$ tsp dried thyme
1 tbsp tomato purée
125 g/4 oz Spanish air-dried
ham, diced
12 black olives
2 tbsp freshly chopped parsley

Rinse the chicken and dry with kitchen paper. Put the flour in a polythene bag, season with salt and pepper and add the chicken. Twist the bag to seal, then shake to coat the chicken. Heat 2 tablespoons of the oil in a large saucepan over a medium-high heat.

Add the chicken and cook for about 5–8 minutes until browned. Using a slotted spoon, place in the cooking dish. Pour in 150 ml/$\frac{1}{4}$ pint of the stock and cover with the lid. Switch the cooker to high and cook for 3 hours.

Add the remaining olive oil to the cleaned saucepan; add the onion and peppers. Cook, stirring, for 5 minutes. Stir in the garlic and chorizo and continue to cook for a further 3 minutes. Add the rice and cook for 1 minute, stirring, until lightly coated in the oil.

Stir in the remaining stock, crushed chillies, thyme, tomato purée and salt and pepper; boil. Remove the chicken from the slow cooker and spoon the rice mixture over the base.

Return the chicken to the dish and re-cover. Continue to cook on high for 45 minutes, or until the chicken and rice are cooked. Switch the slow cooker off and stir in the ham, black olives and half the parsley. Leave covered for 10–15 minutes, or switch the slow cooker to low and cook for a further 30 minutes. Sprinkle with the remaining parsley and serve immediately.

Calypso Chicken

Serves 4–6

2 onions
2 tbsp groundnut oil
450 g/1 lb skinless, boneless
chicken breast, diced
2–4 garlic cloves, peeled
and sliced
1–2 chillies, deseeded and sliced
1 tsp ground coriander
1 tsp ground cumin
1 tsp turmeric
1 tsp ground allspice
600 ml/1 pint chicken stock
1 large red pepper, deseeded
and diced
1 green pepper, deseeded and diced
15 g/½ oz coconut chips, toasted, or
1 tbsp freshly chopped coriander,
to garnish
freshly cooked rice, to serve

Peel the onions and, keeping the root intact, cut into thin wedges. Heat the oil in a heavy-based saucepan, add the chicken and brown on all sides. Remove from the pan and place in the cooking dish.

Add the onions, garlic and chillies to the pan and fry for 5–8 minutes until lightly browned. Sprinkle in all the spices and cook, stirring, for 2 minutes.

Add the stock to the pan and bring to the boil, then carefully transfer to the cooking dish. Cover with the lid and switch the slow cooker to high. Cook for 3 hours.

Stir in the peppers and continue to cook for 45–60 minutes, or until the chicken is thoroughly cooked. Spoon into a warmed serving dish, sprinkle with toasted coconut or chopped coriander and serve with rice.

New Orleans Jambalaya

Serves 6–8

2 dried bay leaves
1 tsp salt
2 tsp cayenne pepper
2 tsp dried oregano
1 tsp each ground white/black pepper
3 tbsp vegetable oil
125 g/4 oz ham
225 g/8 oz smoked pork sausage chunks
2 large onions, peeled and chopped
4 celery stalks, chopped
2 green peppers, deseeded and chopped
2 garlic cloves, peeled and chopped
350 g/12 oz boneless, skinless chicken, diced
400 g can chopped tomatoes
750–900 ml/1^1/$_4$–1^1/$_2$ pints fish stock
400 g/14 oz easy-cook white long-grain rice
4 spring onions, coarsely chopped
275 g/10 oz raw prawns, peeled
250 g/9 oz white crab meat

Mix all the seasoning ingredients together in a small bowl and reserve. Heat 2 tablespoons of the oil in a large, flameproof casserole dish or frying pan over a medium heat. Add the ham and sausage and cook, stirring frequently, for 7–8 minutes until golden.

Remove from the pan and place in the cooking dish. Add the onions, celery and peppers to the casserole dish or frying pan and cook for about 4 minutes until softened, stirring occasionally. Stir in the garlic, then, using a slotted spoon, transfer all the vegetables to the cooking dish.

Add the chicken pieces to the casserole dish or frying pan and cook for about 4 minutes until beginning to colour, turning once. Stir in the seasoning mix and coat well. Place the chicken into the cooking dish. Add the tomatoes with their juice and 750 ml/1^1/4 pints of the stock to the casserole dish or frying pan and bring to the boil; pour over the chicken. Cover with the lid and switch the slow cooker to high. Cook for 3 hours.

Uncover, stir in the rice, spring onions and prawns and re–cover. Cook for a further 30 minutes. Stir in the rest of the stock and the crab. Cook for 15 minutes, or until the chicken is cooked and the rice tender. Switch the cooker off and rest for 5 minutes before serving.

Chilli Baked Chicken

Serves 4

3 medium-hot fresh red
chillies, deseeded
1/2 tsp ground turmeric
1 tsp cumin seeds
1 tsp coriander seeds
2 garlic cloves, crushed
2.5 cm/1 inch piece fresh root ginger,
peeled and chopped
1 tbsp lemon juice
1 tbsp olive oil
2 tbsp chopped fresh coriander
1/2 tsp salt
freshly ground black pepper
1.4 kg/3 lb oven-ready chicken
15 g/1/2 oz unsalted butter, melted
550 g/1 1/4 lb butternut squash
fresh parsley and coriander
sprigs, to garnish

To serve
4 baked potatoes
seasonal green vegetables

Roughly chop the chillies and put in a food processor with the turmeric, cumin seeds, coriander seeds, garlic, ginger, lemon juice, olive oil, coriander, salt, pepper and 2 tablespoons cold water. Blend to a paste, leaving the ingredients still slightly chunky.

Starting at the neck end of the chicken, gently ease up the skin to loosen it from the breast. Reserve 3 tablespoons of the paste. Push the remaining paste over the chicken breast under the skin, spreading it evenly.

Put the chicken into the cooking dish. Mix the reserved chilli paste with the melted butter. Use 1 tablespoon to brush evenly over the chicken and add 4 tablespoons water. Cover with the lid and switch the slow cooker to high. Cook for 1 hour.

Meanwhile, halve, peel and scoop out the seeds from the butternut squash. Cut into large chunks and mix in the remaining chilli paste and butter mixture. Arrange the butternut squash around the chicken. Continue to cook on high for 3–5 hours until the chicken is fully cooked and the juices run clear. Garnish with parsley and coriander. Serve hot with baked potatoes and green vegetables.

Chicken ❧ White Wine Risotto

Serves 4–6

2 tbsp oil
125 g/4 oz unsalted butter
2 shallots, peeled and
finely chopped
300 g/11 oz easy-cook or
Arborio rice
300 ml/½ pint dry white wine
750 ml/1¼ pints chicken
stock, heated
350 g/12 oz skinless chicken breast fillets,
thinly sliced
50 g/2 oz Parmesan
cheese, grated
2 tbsp freshly chopped dill
or parsley
salt and freshly ground
black pepper

Heat half the oil and half the butter in a large, heavy-based saucepan over a medium-high heat. Add the shallots and cook for 2 minutes, or until softened, stirring frequently. Add the rice and cook for 2–3 minutes, stirring frequently, until the rice is translucent and well coated.

Pour in the wine and 150 ml/¼ pint of the stock, then bring to the boil. It will bubble and steam rapidly. When it has subsided, transfer to the cooking dish. Wipe the pan clean and heat the remaining oil. Add the chicken to the saucepan and cook for 5 minutes, or until sealed, turning the chicken over at least once.

Add the chicken to the cooking dish together with most of the stock. Cover with the lid. Switch the slow cooker to high and cook for 2 hours. Stir once during cooking, adding the remaining stock if it is becoming dry.

Switch the slow cooker to auto and stir in the remaining butter with the Parmesan cheese, half the chopped herbs and seasoning to taste. Cook for 30 minutes. Switch the cooker off and leave to stand for 10 minutes. Spoon into warmed shallow bowls and sprinkle each with the remaining chopped herbs. Serve immediately.

Saffron Chicken with Onions

Serves 4–6

1.6 kg/3^1/$_2$ lb oven-ready chicken, preferably free range
75 g/3 oz butter, softened
^{1}/$_2$ tsp saffron strands, lightly toasted
grated zest of 1 lemon
2 tbsp freshly chopped flat-leaf parsley
2 tbsp extra virgin olive oil
450 g/1 lb onions, peeled and cut into thin wedges
8–12 garlic cloves, peeled
1 tsp cumin seeds
^{1}/$_2$ tsp ground cinnamon
50 g/2 oz pine nuts
50 g/2 oz sultanas
salt and freshly ground black pepper
150 ml/^{1}/$_4$ pint chicken stock
fresh flat-leaf parsley sprig, to garnish

Using your fingertips, gently loosen the skin from the chicken breast by sliding your hand between the skin and flesh. Cream together 50 g/2 oz of the butter with the saffron strands, the lemon zest and half the parsley until smooth. Push the butter under the skin. Spread over the breast and the top of the thighs with your fingers. Pull the neck skin to tighten the skin over the breast and tuck under the bird, then secure with a cocktail stick.

Heat the olive oil and remaining butter in a large, heavy-based frying pan and cook the onions and garlic cloves for 5 minutes, or until the onions are soft. Stir in the cumin seeds, cinnamon, pine nuts and sultanas and cook for 2 minutes. Season to taste with salt and pepper and place in the cooking dish. Stir in the stock. Place the chicken, breast side down, on top of the onions, cover with the lid and switch the slow cooker to high.

Cook for 4–5 hours until the chicken is thoroughly cooked and the juices run clear. Turn the chicken over if liked halfway through the cooking time. Switch the slow cooker off and leave to rest for 15 minutes. Sprinkle with the remaining parsley. Garnish with a parsley sprig and serve immediately with the onions and garlic.

Creamy Chicken & Rice Pilaf

Serves 4–6

50 g/2 oz butter
100 g/3½ oz flaked almonds
75 g/3 oz shelled pistachio nuts
4–6 chicken breast fillets,
each cut into 4 pieces
2 tbsp vegetable oil
2 medium onions, thinly sliced
2 garlic cloves, finely chopped
2.5 cm/1 inch piece fresh root
ginger, finely chopped
6 green cardamom pods, crushed
4–6 whole cloves
2 bay leaves
1 tsp ground coriander
½ tsp cayenne pepper
salt and freshly ground black pepper
225 g/8 oz easy-cook basmati rice
600 ml/1 pint chicken stock
225 ml/8 fl oz natural yogurt
3 tbsp ground almonds
225 ml/8 fl oz double cream
225 g/8 oz seedless green grapes
2 tbsp chopped coriander or mint

Heat the butter in a large, deep frying pan over a medium-high heat. Add the almonds and pistachios and cook for 1–2 minutes, stirring constantly, until golden. Using a slotted spoon, remove and reserve.

Add the chicken pieces to the pan and cook for 5 minutes, or until sealed, turning once. Remove from the pan and place in the cooking dish. Add the oil to the pan and cook the onions for 5 minutes, stirring frequently. Stir in the garlic, ginger and spices, then the rice and stock. Bring to the boil and cook for 2 minutes.

Pour the rice mixture over the chicken, cover with the lid and cook on high for 3 hours. Stir in the yogurt and ground almonds with the cream. Re-cover and continue to cook on high for 30 minutes.

Switch the cooker off and stir in the grapes and half the herbs. Leave for 10 minutes and sprinkle with the almonds and pistachio nuts and remaining herbs, then serve.

Chicken Gumbo

Serves 4

8 small skinless chicken portions
1 tbsp olive oil
15 g/¹/₂ oz unsalted butter
1 onion, peeled and chopped
2–3 garlic cloves, peeled
and chopped
1–2 red chillies, deseeded
and chopped
2 celery stalks, trimmed
and sliced
1 red pepper, deseeded
and chopped
225 g/8 oz okra, trimmed
and sliced
4 spicy sausages
2 tbsp plain flour
1.7 litres/3 pints chicken stock
few dashes Tabasco sauce
6 spring onions, trimmed
and chopped
2 x 250 g/9 oz packets precooked
basmati rice, to serve

Rinse the chicken portions and pat dry on absorbent kitchen paper. Heat the oil and butter in a large, heavy-based saucepan, add the chicken and fry, in batches, for 8–10 minutes until lightly browned. Remove with a slotted spoon or metal tongs and reserve.

Add all the vegetables to the pan and fry for 8 minutes, or until the vegetables are beginning to soften. Remove with a slotted spoon and reserve. Add the sausages to the pan and cook for 5–8 minutes until browned all over, then remove and cut each sausage in half. Add half the browned vegetables to the pan and sprinkle in the flour. Cook for 2 minutes, then gradually stir in the stock.

Bring to the boil, then transfer to the cooking dish together with the chicken and sausages. Cover with the lid and switch the slow cooker to high. Cook for 3 hours.

Add the remaining vegetables together with a few dashes of Tabasco. Re-cover with the lid and cook on high for 30 minutes. Stir in the spring onions. Heat the rice according to the packet instructions, then place a serving in a deep bowl. Ladle a portion of the gumbo over the rice and serve.

Lemon Chicken Rice

Serves 4

2 tbsp sunflower oil
4 chicken leg portions
1 medium onion, peeled and chopped
1–2 garlic cloves, peeled and crushed
1 tbsp curry powder
25 g/1 oz butter
225 g/8 oz easy-cook white long-grain rice
1 lemon, preferably unwaxed, sliced
600–750 ml/1–1 1/4 pints chicken stock
salt and freshly ground black pepper
2 tbsp flaked, toasted almonds
fresh coriander sprigs, to garnish

Heat the oil in a large frying pan, add the chicken legs and cook, turning, until sealed and golden all over. Using a slotted spoon, remove the chicken from the pan and place in the cooking dish.

Add the onion and garlic to the oil remaining in the frying pan and cook for 5 minutes, or until just beginning to brown. Sprinkle in the curry powder and cook, stirring, for a further 1 minute. Sprinkle over the chicken and cover with the lid. Switch the slow cooker to high and cook for 3 hours.

Wipe the frying pan clean, then heat and add the butter. Sprinkle in the rice and cook, stirring, to ensure that all the grains are coated in the melted butter. Stir in 600 ml/1 pint of the stock and bring to the boil. Carefully add to the cooking dish together with the lemon slices, spooning it round and over the chicken. Season to taste with salt and pepper.

Re-cover with the lid and cook on high for 1 hour. Check if the rice is becoming dry and, if so, add the remaining stock and continue to cook for a further 30 minutes, or until the rice is tender and the chicken is cooked thoroughly. Serve sprinkled with the toasted flaked almonds and sprigs of coriander.

Chicken Cacciatore

Serves 4

2–3 tbsp olive oil
125 g/4 oz pancetta or streaky bacon, diced
1.4 kg/3 lb chicken,
cut into 8 pieces
25 g/1 oz plain flour
salt and freshly ground
black pepper
2 garlic cloves, peeled and chopped
125 ml/4 fl oz red wine
400 g can chopped tomatoes
150 ml/¼ pint chicken stock
12 small onions,
peeled1 bay leaf
1 tsp brown sugar
1 tsp dried oregano
1 green pepper, deseeded
and chopped
225 g/8 oz chestnut or field mushrooms,
thickly sliced
2 tbsp freshly chopped parsley
freshly cooked tagliatelle, to serve

Heat 1 tablespoon of the olive oil in a large, deep frying pan and add the diced pancetta or bacon and fry for 2–3 minutes until crisp and golden brown. Using a slotted spoon, transfer the pancetta or bacon to the cooking dish.

Lightly rinse the chicken and dry on absorbent kitchen paper. Season the flour with salt and pepper, then use to coat the chicken. Heat the remaining oil in the pan and brown the chicken pieces on all sides for about 15 minutes. Remove from the pan and add to the cooking dish.

Stir the garlic into the pan and cook for about 30 seconds. Add the red wine and cook, stirring and scraping any browned bits from the base of the pan. Allow the wine to boil until it is reduced by half. Add the tomatoes, stock, onions, bay leaf, brown sugar and oregano and stir well. Season to taste.

Bring the tomato mixture to the boil, then pour over the chicken. Cover with the lid and switch the slow cooker to high. Cook for 2 hours. Stir in the pepper and mushrooms, re-cover and cook for a further 1 hour, or until the chicken and vegetables are tender. Stir in the chopped parsley and serve immediately with freshly cooked tagliatelle.

Chicken ❧ Papaya Curry

Serves 4–6

2 tbsp groundnut oil

450 g/1 lb skinless, boneless chicken, diced

2 red onions, peeled and cut into wedges

4 garlic cloves, peeled and sliced

5 cm/2 inch piece fresh root ginger, grated

2 tsp chilli powder

1 tsp ground allspice

1 tbsp mild curry paste

1–2 limes (preferably organic)

few curry leaves

300 ml/1/2 pint chicken stock

300 g/11 oz carrots, sliced

1 large papaya, ripe but still firm

1 green pepper, deseeded and chopped

2 small bananas, sliced

To serve

freshly cooked rice

freshly cooked peas

Heat the oil in a heavy-based saucepan, add the chicken and brown on all sides. Remove and reserve. Add the onions, garlic and ginger to the pan and fry for 5 minutes. Add the spices and curry paste and cook for 5 minutes, stirring. Return the chicken to the pan and stir until the chicken is coated in the spices.

Finely grate the zest from the limes to give 1 tablespoon. Squeeze out the juice to give 3 tablespoons. Stir in the curry leaves, lime zest and juice and stock. Add the carrots and bring to the boil. Carefully transfer to the cooking dish and switch the slow cooker to high. Cook for 3 1/2 hours.

Peel the papaya, then remove the seeds and chop the flesh. Add the papaya flesh to the cooking dish with the green pepper and bananas and cook for a further 30 minutes, or until the chicken is cooked. Spoon into a warmed serving dish and serve with rice and peas.

Chicken with Porcini & Cream

Serves 4

2 tbsp olive oil
4 boneless chicken breasts, skinned if preferred
2 garlic cloves, peeled and crushed
150 ml/¼ pint dry vermouth or dry white wine
salt and freshly ground black pepper
25 g/1 oz butter
450 g/1 lb porcini or wild mushrooms, thickly sliced
1 tbsp freshly chopped oregano
fresh basil sprigs, to garnish (optional)
freshly cooked rice, to serve

Heat the olive oil in a large, heavy-based frying pan, then add the chicken breasts and fry for 5–8 minutes until they are browned. Remove the chicken breasts and place in the cooking dish. Add the garlic, stir into the juices and cook for 1 minute.

Pour the vermouth or white wine into the pan and season to taste with salt and pepper. Bring to the boil, then carefully transfer to the cooking dish. Cover with the lid and switch the slow cooker to high. Cook for 2–2½ hours.

Wipe the frying pan clean, then add the butter and heat. Add the sliced porcini or wild mushrooms and cook for 5 minutes.

Add all the mushrooms and any juices to the chicken together with seasoning to taste. Re-cover and cook for a further 30 minutes, or until the chicken is thoroughly cooked. Transfer to a large serving plate and garnish with sprigs of fresh basil, if liked. Serve immediately with rice.

Chicken Chasseur

Serves 4

1 whole chicken, about 1.4 kg/3 lb in weight,
jointed into 4 or 8 portions
1 tbsp olive oil
15 g/1/2 oz unsalted butter
12 baby onions, peeled
2–4 garlic cloves, peeled
and sliced
2 celery stalks, sliced
175 g/6 oz closed-cup mushrooms
2 tbsp plain flour
300 ml/1/2 pint dry white wine
2 tbsp tomato purée
450 ml/3/4 pint chicken stock
salt and freshly ground black pepper
1 tsp dried tarragon or few fresh
tarragon sprigs
350 g/12 oz sweet potatoes,
peeled and cut into chunks
300 g/11 oz shelled fresh or
frozen broad beans
1 tbsp freshly chopped tarragon, to garnish

Skin the chicken, if preferred, and rinse lightly. Pat dry on absorbent kitchen paper. Heat the oil and butter in a heavy-based frying pan, add the chicken portions and fry for 5–8 minutes, in batches, until browned all over. Remove with a slotted spoon and place in the cooking dish.

Add the onions, garlic and celery to the frying pan and cook for 5 minutes, or until golden. Cut the mushrooms in half if large, then add to the pan and cook for 2 minutes. Sprinkle in the flour and cook for 2 minutes, then gradually stir in the wine.

Blend the tomato purée with a little of the stock in a small bowl, then stir into the pan together with the remaining stock, seasoning to taste, and the dried or fresh tarragon. Bring to the boil, stirring constantly.

Pour the sauce over the chicken and cover with the lid. Switch the slow cooker to high and cook for 3 hours.

Stir in the sweet potatoes. Re-cover with the lid and continue to cook for a further 30 minutes. Add the broad beans and cook for a further 30 minutes, or until the chicken and vegetables are cooked. Serve sprinkled with freshly chopped tarragon.

Orange-flavoured Chicken

Serves 6

1 small orange, thinly sliced
50 g/2 oz sugar
1.4 kg/3 lb oven-ready chicken
1 small bunch fresh coriander
1 small bunch fresh mint
2 tbsp olive oil
1 tsp Chinese five-spice powder
1/2 tsp paprika
1 tsp fennel seeds, crushed
salt and freshly ground
black pepper
150 ml/1/4 pint orange juice
fresh coriander sprigs,
to garnish
freshly cooked vegetables,
to serve

Place the orange slices in a small saucepan, cover with water, bring to the boil, then simmer for 2 minutes and drain. Place the sugar in a clean saucepan with 150 ml/1/4 pint fresh water. Stir over a low heat until the sugar dissolves, then bring to the boil, add the drained orange slices and simmer for 10 minutes. Remove from the heat and leave in the syrup until cold.

Remove any excess fat from inside the chicken. Starting at the neck end, carefully loosen the skin of the chicken over the breast and legs, without tearing. Push the orange slices under the loosened skin with the coriander and mint. Mix together the olive oil, Chinese five-spice powder, paprika and crushed fennel seeds and season to taste with salt and pepper.

Brush the chicken skin generously with this mixture and place in the cooking dish. Pour round the orange juice. Cover with the lid and switch the slow cooker to high.

Cook for 4 hours, or until the juices run clear when a skewer is inserted into the thickest part of the thigh. Switch the cooker off and leave to rest for 10 minutes. Garnish with sprigs of fresh coriander and serve with freshly cooked vegetables.

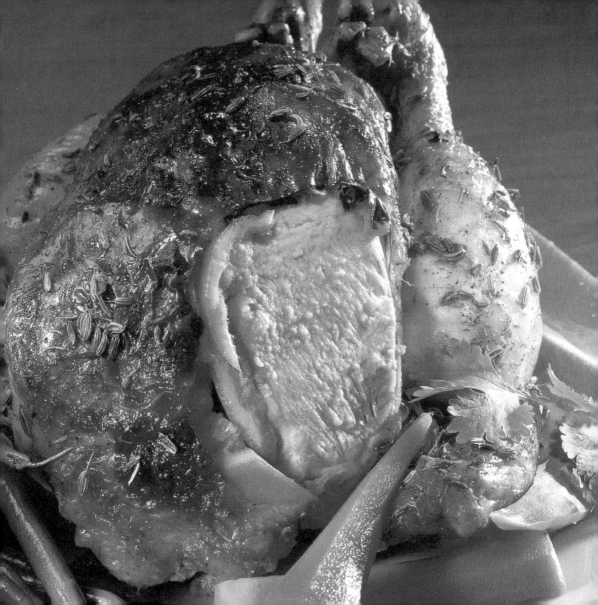

Bengali Chicken Curry

Serves 4

2–3 red chillies, deseeded
and chopped
3 garlic cloves, peeled
and chopped
5 cm/2 inch piece root ginger,
peeled and grated
4 shallots, peeled and chopped
1 tsp turmeric
250 ml/8 fl oz water
450 g/1 lb skinless,
boneless chicken
2 tbsp vegetable oil or ghee
few curry leaves
1 tbsp freshly chopped coriander

To serve
Indian-style bread
salad

Place the chillies, garlic, ginger, shallots, turmeric and 150 ml/¼ pint of the water in a food processor until smooth, then pour into a shallow dish.

Lightly rinse the chicken and pat dry with absorbent kitchen paper. Cut the chicken into thin strips, then add them to the spice mixture. Cover and leave to marinate in the refrigerator for 15–30 minutes, stirring occasionally, or longer if time permits.

Heat the oil or ghee in a heavy-based frying pan, then, using a slotted spoon, remove the chicken from the marinade, reserving the marinade. Cook the chicken for 5 minutes, or until sealed.

Remove the chicken and place in the cooking dish. Pour the reserved marinade over the chicken and add the curry leaves and the remaining water. Cover with the lid and switch the slow cooker to high.

Cook for 3 hours, or until the chicken is thoroughly cooked. Spoon into a warmed serving dish, sprinkle with the chopped coriander and serve with bread and salad.

Thai-flavoured Chicken

Serves 4

1 tsp cumin seeds
1 tsp mustard seeds
1 tsp coriander seeds
1 tsp turmeric
1 bird's-eye chilli, deseeded
and finely chopped
1 tbsp freshly grated
root ginger
2 garlic cloves, peeled and
finely chopped
125 ml/4 fl oz double cream
8 skinless chicken thighs
2 tbsp groundnut oil
1 onion, peeled and
finely sliced
200 ml/7 fl oz chicken stock
salt and freshly ground
black pepper
4 tbsp freshly chopped coriander
2 spring onions, shredded,
to garnish
freshly cooked Thai fragrant
rice, to serve

Heat a wok or heavy-based frying pan and add the cumin seeds, mustard seeds and coriander seeds. Dry-fry over a low to medium heat for 2 minutes, or until the fragrance becomes stronger and the seeds start to pop. Add the turmeric and leave to cool. Grind the spices in a pestle and mortar or blend to a fine powder in a food processor.

Mix the chilli, ginger, garlic and the cream together in a small bowl, add the ground spices and mix. Place the chicken thighs in a shallow dish and spread the spice paste over the thighs.

Heat the wok or frying pan and add the oil and, when hot, add the onion and fry until golden brown. Add the chicken and spice paste. Cook for 5–6 minutes, stirring occasionally, until evenly coloured. Add the stock and season to taste with salt and pepper. Transfer to the cooking dish.

Cover with the lid and switch the slow cooker to high. Cook for 3–4 hours until the chicken is thoroughly cooked. Stir in the chopped coriander and serve immediately with the freshly cooked rice sprinkled with shredded spring onions.

Chicken ❦ Chickpea Korma

Serves 4–6

350 g/12 oz skinless, boneless chicken
2 tbsp vegetable oil
2 onions, peeled and cut
into wedges
2–4 garlic cloves, peeled
and chopped
2–3 tbsp Korma curry paste
1 tsp garam masala
$^{1}/_{2}$–1 tsp ground cloves
450 ml/$^{3}/_{4}$ pint chicken stock
225 g/8 oz ripe tomatoes,
peeled and chopped
400 g/14 oz can chickpeas,
drained and rinsed
4 tbsp double cream
6 spring onions, trimmed and
diagonally sliced
Indian-style bread, to serve

Cut the chicken into small strips and reserve. Heat the oil in a heavy-based frying pan, add the chicken and cook, stirring, for 3 minutes, or until sealed. Remove and place in the cooking dish.

Add the onion and garlic to the pan and fry gently for 5 minutes, or until the onion has begun to soften. Add the curry paste, garam masala and ground cloves and cook, stirring, for 2 minutes. Pour the sauce over the chicken and stir.

Stir the stock, tomatoes and chickpeas into the chicken and onion mixture, then cover with the lid. Switch the slow cooker to high and cook for 3 hours, or until the chicken is thoroughly cooked. Stir in the cream. Spoon into a warmed serving dish, sprinkle with the spring onions and serve with Indian-style bread.

Potato-stuffed Poussin

Serves 4

4 oven-ready poussins
salt and freshly ground
black pepper
1 lemon, cut into quarters
450 g/1 lb floury potatoes, peeled
and cut into 4 cm/
1½ inch pieces
1 tbsp freshly chopped thyme
or rosemary
3–4 tbsp olive oil
4 garlic cloves, unpeeled and lightly
smashed
8 slices streaky bacon or
Parma ham
125 ml/4 fl oz white wine
2 spring onions, trimmed and thinly sliced
2 tbsp double cream or
crème fraîche
lemon wedges, to garnish

Rinse the poussin cavities and pat dry with absorbent kitchen paper. Season the cavities with salt and pepper and a squeeze of lemon. Push a lemon quarter into each cavity. Put the potatoes in a saucepan of lightly salted water and bring to the boil. Reduce the heat to low and simmer for 10 minutes. Drain and cool slightly. Sprinkle the chopped herbs over the potatoes and drizzle with 2–3 tablespoons of the oil.

Spoon half the potatoes into the poussin cavities; do not pack too tightly. Rub each poussin with a little more oil and season with pepper. Place the poussins in the cooking dish and cover with the lid. Spoon the remaining potatoes around the edge. Sprinkle over the garlic.

Cover with the lid, switch the slow cooker to high and cook for 3 hours. Lay the bacon slices over the breast of each poussin and continue to cook for 1 hour, or until the poussins are cooked through.

Transfer the poussins and potatoes to a serving dish and cover with foil. Skim off the fat from the juices, pour into a small saucepan and heat. Stir the wine and spring onions into the pan. Bring to the boil, then whisk in the cream or crème fraîche and bubble for 1 minute, or until thickened. Garnish the poussins with lemon wedges and serve with the creamy gravy.

North Indian Chicken

ℰ

Serves 4–6

8 small chicken thighs
3–4 tbsp vegetable oil or ghee
2 onions, peeled and cut
into wedges
2–3 garlic cloves,
peeled and sliced
2 green chillies, deseeded
and sliced
2 red chillies, deseeded
and sliced
2–3 tbsp Madras curry
paste, or to taste
450 ml/³⁄4 pint water
few curry leaves
2 tbsp lemon juice
2 tbsp sesame seeds
fresh coriander sprigs,
to garnish
freshly cooked rice, to serve

Skin the chicken, if preferred, then rinse and pat dry with absorbent kitchen paper. Heat 2 tablespoons of the oil or ghee in a large, deep frying pan, add the chicken and brown on all sides. Remove and reserve.

Add a further tablespoon of the oil, if necessary, to the pan, then add the onions, garlic and half the chillies and fry for 5 minutes, or until beginning to soften. Stir in the curry paste and cook for 2 minutes, stirring frequently. Take care not to burn the mixture.

Take off the heat, return the chicken to the pan and roll around in the paste until lightly coated. Stir in the water. Return to the heat and bring to the boil, then carefully transfer to the cooking dish. Add the curry leaves, cover with the lid and switch the slow cooker to high. Cook for 4 hours, or until the chicken is thoroughly cooked.

Switch the slow cooker off, pour the lemon juice over the chicken and leave to rest for 10 minutes. Just before serving, heat the remaining oil in a small frying pan and gently fry the rest of the chillies and the sesame seeds until the chillies have become crisp and the seeds toasted. Serve the chicken on rice sprinkled with the chillies and sesame seeds and garnished with coriander sprigs.

Persian Chicken Pilaf

꡴

Serves 4–6

2–3 tbsp vegetable oil
700 g/1½ lb boneless, skinless
chicken pieces (breast and thighs),
cut into 2.5 cm/1 inch pieces
2 medium onions, peeled and
coarsely chopped
1 tsp ground cumin
200 g/7 oz easy-cook long-grain white rice
1 tbsp tomato purée
1 tsp saffron strands
salt and freshly ground
black pepper
100 ml/3 ½ fl oz pomegranate juice
750 ml/1¼ pints chicken stock
125 g/4 oz ready-to-eat dried apricots or
prunes, halved
2 tbsp raisins
2 tbsp freshly chopped
mint or parsley
pomegranate seeds, to garnish (optional)

Heat half the oil in a large, heavy-based saucepan over a medium-high heat. Cook the chicken pieces, in batches, until lightly browned. Remove from the pan and place in the cooking dish. Pour in 150 ml/¼ pint of the stock. Cover with the lid and switch the slow cooker to high. Cook for 3 hours.

Add the remaining oil to the cleaned saucepan together with the onions. Reduce the heat to medium and cook for 3–5 minutes, stirring frequently, until the onions begin to soften. Add the cumin and rice and stir to coat the rice.

Cook for about 2 minutes until the rice is golden and translucent. Stir in the tomato purée and the saffron strands, then season to taste with salt and pepper. Add the pomegranate juice and remaining stock and bring to the boil, stirring once or twice. Add the apricots or prunes and raisins and stir gently.

Remove the chicken from the slow cooker and place the rice mixture over the base. Return the chicken and re-cover with the lid. Continue to cook on high for a further 45 minutes, or until the chicken is thoroughly cooked. Turn into a shallow serving dish and sprinkle with the chopped mint or parsley. Serve immediately, garnished with pomegranate seeds, if using.

Duck in Black Bean Sauce

Serves 4

450 g/1 lb duck breast, skinned
1 tbsp light soy sauce
1 tbsp Chinese rice wine
or dry sherry
2.5 cm/1 inch piece fresh
root ginger
3 garlic cloves
2 spring onions
2 tbsp Chinese preserved
black beans
1 tbsp groundnut or vegetable oil
150 ml/¼ pint chicken stock
shredded spring onions,
to garnish
freshly cooked noodles, to serve

Using a sharp knife, trim the duck breasts, removing any fat. Slice thickly and place in a shallow dish. Mix together the soy sauce and Chinese rice wine or sherry and pour over the duck. Leave to marinate in the refrigerator for 1 hour, then drain and discard the marinade.

Peel the ginger and chop finely. Peel the garlic cloves and either chop finely or crush. Trim the roots from the spring onions, discard the outer leaves and chop. Finely chop the black beans.

Heat a wok or large frying pan, add the oil and, when very hot, add the ginger, garlic, spring onions and black beans and fry for 30 seconds. Add the drained duck and fry for 3–5 minutes until the duck is browned.

Add the chicken stock and bring to the boil. Carefully transfer to the cooking dish and cover with the lid. Switch the slow cooker to auto and cook for 1 hour; switch to low and cook for 2–3 hours until the duck is cooked and the sauce is reduced and thickened. Tip onto a bed of freshly cooked noodles, garnish with spring onion shreds and serve immediately.

Pheasant with Sage & Blueberries

Serves 4

3 tbsp olive oil
3 shallots, peeled and coarsely chopped
2 fresh sage sprigs, coarsely chopped
1 bay leaf
1 lemon, halved
salt and freshly ground black pepper
2 pheasants or guinea fowl, rinsed and dried
125 g/4 oz blueberries
4 slices Parma ham or bacon
125 ml/4 fl oz vermouth or dry white wine
200 ml/¹⁄₃ pint chicken stock
3 tbsp double cream or butter (optional)
1 tbsp brandy
roast potatoes, to serve

Place the oil, shallots, sage and bay leaf in a bowl with the juice from the lemon halves. Season with salt and pepper. Place the squeezed lemon halves into the birds with 75 g/3 oz of the blueberries, then rub the birds with the marinade and leave to marinate in the refrigerator for 2–3 hours, basting occasionally.

Remove the birds from the marinade and cover each with 2 slices of Parma ham. Tie the legs of each bird with string and place in the cooking dish. Pour over the marinade and add the vermouth. Cover and switch the slow cooker to auto. Cook for 3–4 hours until the juices run clear when a thigh is pierced with a sharp knife or skewer.

Place on a warm serving plate, cover with foil and discard the string; keep warm. Pour the juices left in the cooking dish into a small saucepan and skim off any surface fat. Heat gently. Add the stock to the saucepan and bring to the boil. Boil until slightly reduced. Whisk in the cream or butter, if using, and simmer until thickened, whisking constantly.

Stir in the brandy and strain into a gravy jug. Add the remaining blueberries and keep warm. Using a sharp carving knife, cut each of the birds in half and arrange on the plate with the crispy Parma ham. Serve immediately with roast potatoes and the gravy.

Vegetarian

Meals

The recipes in this chapter allow those often forgotten–about vegetables, often just relegated to side dishes, to be the stars of the show. Stuffed Butternut Squash is a dish too good not to be tried; while Vegetarian Cassoulet is the ultimate comforting, winter warmer dish. Spicy Creamy Vegetable Korma will be proof that vegetables can be far from dull!

Bean ❧ Mushroom Cassoulet

Serves 6

125 g/4 oz dried haricot beans, soaked overnight
2 tbsp olive oil
2 garlic cloves, peeled and chopped
225 g/8 oz baby onions, peeled and halved
2 carrots, peeled and diced
2 celery stalks, trimmed and finely chopped
1 red pepper, deseeded and chopped
175 g/6 oz mixed mushrooms, sliced
1 tbsp each freshly chopped rosemary, thyme and sage
150 ml/1/4 pint red wine
4 tbsp tomato purée
1 tbsp dark soy sauce
salt and freshly ground black pepper
50 g/2 oz fresh breadcrumbs
1 tbsp freshly chopped parsley
basil sprigs, to garnish

Drain the haricot beans and place in a saucepan with 1.1 litres/2 pints fresh water. Bring to the boil and boil rapidly for 10 minutes. Place in the cooking dish, cover with the lid and switch the slow cooker to auto. Cook for 1 hour, then cool slightly before draining and reserving 300 ml/1/2 pint of the liquid.

Heat 1 tablespoon of the oil in a saucepan and add the garlic, onions, carrots, celery and red pepper. Cook gently for 5 minutes. Add the mushrooms and cook for a further 3 minutes, or until starting to soften; stir in the herbs. Stir in the red wine and boil rapidly for about 5 minutes until reduced and syrupy. Stir in the reserved beans and their liquid, tomato purée and soy sauce. Season to taste with salt and pepper.

Spoon into the cooking dish. Mix together the breadcrumbs and parsley with the remaining oil. Scatter this mixture evenly over the top of the cassoulet. Cover with the lid and switch the slow cooker to low. Cook for 6 hours.

Preheat the grill and remove the lid from the slow cooker. Place under the grill and cook for 5–6 minutes, turning the dish until the top is crisp. Serve immediately, garnished with basil sprigs.

Vegetable ❧ Herb Risotto

Serves 2–3

750 ml/1¼ pints
vegetable stock
125 g/4 oz asparagus tips, trimmed
125 g/4 oz baby carrots, scrubbed
50 g/2 oz peas,
fresh or frozen
50 g/2 oz fine French
beans, trimmed
1 tbsp olive oil
1 onion, peeled and finely chopped
1 garlic clove, peeled and finely chopped
2 tsp freshly chopped thyme
225 g/8 oz easy-cook or Arborio rice
150 ml/¼ pint white wine
1 tbsp each freshly chopped basil,
chives and parsley
finely grated zest of ½ lemon
3 tbsp half-fat crème fraîche
salt and freshly ground black pepper

Bring the vegetable stock to the boil in a large saucepan and add the asparagus, baby carrots, peas and beans. Bring the stock back to the boil and remove the vegetables at once using a slotted spoon. Rinse under cold running water and reserve. Keep the stock hot.

Heat the oil in a large, deep frying pan and add the onion. Cook over a medium heat for 4–5 minutes until starting to brown. Add the garlic and thyme and cook for a further few seconds. Add the rice and stir well for a minute until the rice is hot and coated in oil.

Add the white wine and stir constantly until the wine is almost completely absorbed by the rice. Spoon into the cooking dish and stir in the stock together with the vegetables.

Cover with the lid and switch the slow cooker to high. Cook for 1½ hours, or until the rice is tender but still retains a bite, *al dente*. Switch the slow cooker off and stir in the herbs, lemon zest and crème fraîche. Season to taste with salt and pepper and serve immediately.

Thai Cauliflower ❧ Potato Curry

Serves 4

3 garlic cloves, peeled
and crushed
1 onion, peeled and finely chopped
40 g/1½ oz ground almonds
1 tsp ground coriander
½ tsp ground cumin
½ tsp turmeric
3 tbsp groundnut oil
salt and freshly ground
black pepper
50 g/2 oz creamed coconut, broken
into small pieces
450 g/1 lb new potatoes, scrubbed or peeled
and halved or quartered, depending on size
350 g/12 oz cauliflower florets
200 ml/7 fl oz vegetable stock
1 tbsp mango chutney
fresh coriander sprigs, to garnish
freshly cooked basmati rice,
to serve

Blend the garlic, onion, ground almonds and spices with 2 tablespoons of the oil and salt and pepper to taste in a food processor until a smooth paste is formed. Heat a heavy-based frying pan, add the remaining oil and, when hot, add the spice paste and cook for 3–4 minutes, stirring continuously.

Dissolve the creamed coconut in 6 tablespoons boiling water and add to the frying pan. Pour in the stock, cook for 2–3 minutes, then stir in the potatoes and cauliflower.

Carefully transfer to the cooking dish and cover with the lid. Switch the slow cooker to low and cook for 6–7 hours.

Stir in the mango chutney and cook for a further 1 hour. Tip into a warmed serving dish, garnish with sprigs of fresh coriander and serve immediately with freshly cooked rice.

Baby Onion Risotto

Serves 4

For the baby onions
1 tbsp olive oil
450 g/1 lb baby onions, peeled, and halved if large
pinch sugar
1 tbsp freshly chopped thyme

For the risotto
1 tbsp olive oil
1 small onion, finely chopped
2 garlic cloves, finely chopped
350 g/12 oz easy-cook or Arborio rice
150 ml/1/4 pint red wine
900 ml/1 1/2 pints hot vegetable stock
125 g/4 oz low-fat soft goat's cheese
salt and freshly ground black pepper
fresh thyme sprigs, to garnish
rocket leaves, to serve

For the baby onions, heat the olive oil in a saucepan and add the onions with the sugar. Cover and cook over a low heat, stirring occasionally, for 10 minutes, then place in the cooking dish.

Heat the oil in a large frying pan and add the chopped onion. Cook over a medium heat for 5 minutes until softened. Add the garlic and cook for a further 30 seconds.

Sprinkle in the rice and stir well. Add the red wine and stir constantly until the wine is almost completely absorbed by the rice. Spoon into the cooking dish with the baby onions. Pour in 600 ml/1 pint of the stock and cover with the lid. Switch the slow cooker to high and cook for 1 hour. Stir, adding more stock if becoming dry. Continue to cook for 20–30 minutes until the rice is tender but still retains a bite, *al dente*.

Add the thyme and the goat's cheese to the risotto. Stir well and season to taste with salt and pepper. Garnish with sprigs of fresh thyme. Serve immediately with the rocket leaves.

Vegetarian Cassoulet

Serves 4

225 g/8 oz dried haricot beans,
soaked overnight
2 medium onions
1 bay leaf
1.4 litres/2½ pints cold water
salt and freshly ground
black pepper
5 tsp olive oil
1 large garlic clove, crushed
2 leeks, trimmed and sliced
200 g can chopped tomatoes
1 tsp dark muscovado sugar
1 tbsp freshly chopped thyme
2 tbsp freshly chopped parsley
550 g/1¼ lb large potatoes, peeled and sliced
3 courgettes, trimmed and sliced

For the topping

50 g/2 oz fresh white breadcrumbs
25 g/1 oz Cheddar cheese,
finely grated

Drain the beans, rinse under cold running water and put in a saucepan. Peel one of the onions and add to the beans with the bay leaf. Pour in the water. Bring to a rapid boil and cook for 10 minutes, then turn down the heat, cover and simmer for a further 10 minutes. Drain the beans, reserving the liquor, but discarding the onion and bay leaf.

Peel and chop the remaining onion. Heat the oil in a frying pan and cook the onion with the garlic and leeks for 5 minutes until softened. Stir in the tomatoes, sugar, thyme and parsley. Stir in the beans, with 300 ml/½ pint of the reserved liquor and season to taste.

Layer the potato slices, courgettes and the bean mixture in the cooking dish. To make the topping, mix together the breadcrumbs and cheese and sprinkle over the top. Cover with the lid and switch the slow cooker to low. Cook for 6–8 hours until the vegetables are cooked through.

Preheat the grill and remove the lid from the slow cooker. Place under the grill and cook for 5–6 minutes, turning the dish, until the top is crisp. Serve immediately.

Stuffed Butternut Squash

Serves 4

2 small butternut squash
4 garlic cloves, peeled
and crushed
1 tbsp olive oil
salt and freshly ground
black pepper
1 tbsp walnut or olive oil
4 medium-size leeks, trimmed, cleaned
and thinly sliced
1 tbsp black mustard seeds
300 g can cannellini beans,
drained and rinsed
125 g/4 oz fine French
beans, halved
150 ml/¼ pint vegetable stock
50 g/2 oz rocket
2 tbsp freshly snipped chives
fresh chives, to garnish

To serve

4 tbsp low-fat fromage frais
mixed salad

Cut the butternut squash in half lengthways and scoop out all of the seeds.

Score the squash in a diamond pattern with a sharp knife. Mix the garlic with the olive oil and brush over the cut surfaces of the squash. Season well with salt and pepper.

Heat the oil in a saucepan and fry the leeks and mustard seeds for 5 minutes.

Add the drained cannellini beans, French beans and vegetable stock. Bring to the boil and simmer gently for 5 minutes.

Remove from the heat and stir in the rocket and chives. Season well. Spoon the bean mixture into the halved butternut squash and place in the cooking dish. Cover with the lid and switch the slow cooker to low. Cook for 8–9 hours until the squash is tender. Serve garnished with a few snipped chives and serve immediately with the fromage frais and a mixed salad.

Spiced Tomato Pilaf

Serves 2–3

225 g/8 oz easy-cook basmati rice
40 g/1 1/2 oz unsalted butter
4 green cardamom pods
2 star anise
4 whole cloves
10 black peppercorns
5 cm/2 inch long
cinnamon stick
1 large red onion, peeled
and finely sliced
175 g/6 oz canned
chopped tomatoes
salt and freshly ground
black pepper
fresh coriander sprigs,
to garnish

Wash the rice in several changes of water until the water remains relatively clear. Drain the rice and cover with fresh water. Leave to soak for 30 minutes. Drain well and reserve.

Heat a frying pan, then melt the butter and add the cardamoms, star anise, cloves, black peppercorns and the cinnamon stick. Cook gently for 30 seconds. Increase the heat and add the onion. Fry for 7–8 minutes until tender and starting to brown. Add the drained rice and cook for a further 2–3 minutes.

Blend the tomatoes in a food processor to form a purée and mix with sufficient warm water to make 600 ml/1 pint. Pour this into the pan, season to taste with salt and pepper and bring to the boil.

Carefully transfer to the cooking dish and cover with the lid. Switch the slow cooker to auto and cook for 1 1/2 hours. Remove the lid and fluff up with a fork, then garnish with the sprigs of fresh coriander and serve immediately.

Brown Rice Spiced Pilaf

Serves 4

1 tbsp vegetable oil
1 tbsp blanched almonds,
flaked or chopped
1 onion, peeled and chopped
1 carrot, peeled and diced
225 g/8 oz flat mushrooms,
thickly sliced
1/4 tsp cinnamon
large pinch dried chilli flakes
50 g/2 oz dried apricots,
roughly chopped
25 g/1 oz currants
finely grated zest of 1 orange
350 g/12 oz easy-cook
brown basmati rice
900 ml/1 1/2 pints
vegetable stock
2 tbsp freshly chopped coriander
2 tbsp freshly snipped chives
salt and freshly ground
black pepper
snipped chives, to garnish

Heat the oil in a heavy-based saucepan and add the almonds. Cook for 1–2 minutes until just browning. (Be very careful, as the nuts will burn very easily.)

Add the onion and carrot. Cook for 5 minutes until softened and starting to turn brown. Add the mushrooms and cook for a further 5 minutes, stirring often.

Add the cinnamon and chilli flakes and cook for about 30 seconds before adding the apricots, currants, orange zest and rice.

Stir well and add the stock. Bring to the boil, then carefully transfer to the cooking dish. Cover with the lid and switch the slow cooker to high or auto. Cook on high for 1 1/2 hours, or on auto for 2–3 hours until the rice is tender but still retains a bite, *al dente*.

Stir the coriander and chives into the pilaf and season to taste with salt and pepper. Garnish with the extra chives and serve immediately.

Creamy Vegetable Korma

Serves 4–6

2 tbsp vegetable oil or ghee
1 large onion, peeled and chopped
2 garlic cloves, peeled and crushed
2.5 cm/1 inch piece root ginger,
peeled and grated
4 cardamom pods
2 tsp ground coriander
1 tsp ground cumin
1 tsp ground turmeric
finely grated zest and juice
of ½ lemon
50 g/2 oz ground almonds
400 ml/14 fl oz vegetable stock
450 g/1 lb potatoes,
peeled and diced
450 g/1 lb mixed vegetables, such as cauliflower,
carrots and turnip, cut into chunks
150 ml/¼ pint double cream
3 tbsp freshly chopped coriander
salt and freshly ground
black pepper
naan bread, to serve

Heat the oil or ghee in a large saucepan. Add the onion and cook for 5 minutes. Stir in the garlic and ginger and cook for a further 5 minutes, or until soft and just beginning to colour.

Stir in the cardamom, ground coriander, cumin and turmeric. Continue cooking over a low heat for 1 minute, stirring.

Stir in the lemon zest and juice and the almonds. Blend in the vegetable stock. Slowly bring to the boil, stirring occasionally. Add the potatoes and vegetables and bring back to the boil.

Carefully transfer to the cooking dish. Cover with the lid and switch the slow cooker to low. Cook for 6–7 hours until the vegetables are tender.

Slowly stir in the cream and chopped coriander. Season to taste with salt and pepper. Serve immediately with naan bread.

Three Bean Tagine

Serves 4

few saffron strands
2–3 tbsp olive oil
1 small aubergine, diced
1 onion, peeled and chopped
350 g/12 oz sweet potatoes, peeled
and diced
225 g/8 oz carrots, peeled
and chopped
1 cinnamon stick, bruised
1½ tsp ground cumin
salt and freshly ground
black pepper
600 ml/1 pint vegetable stock
2 fresh mint sprigs
200 g/7 oz can red kidney
beans, drained
300 g/10 oz can haricot
beans, drained
300 g/10 oz can flageolet
beans, drained
1 tbsp freshly chopped mint,
to garnish

Place warm water into a small bowl and sprinkle with the saffron strands. Leave to infuse for at least 10 minutes.

Heat the oil in a large, heavy-based saucepan, add the aubergine and onion and fry for 5 minutes before adding the sweet potatoes, carrots, cinnamon stick and ground cumin. Cook, stirring, until the vegetables are lightly coated in the cumin. Add the saffron with the soaking liquid and season to taste with salt and pepper. Pour in the stock and add the mint sprigs.

Rinse the beans, add to the pan and bring to the boil. Carefully transfer to the cooking dish and cover with the lid. Switch the slow cooker to low and cook for 6 hours, or until the vegetables are tender. Adjust the seasoning to taste, then serve sprinkled with chopped mint.

Light Ratatouille

Serves 4

1 red pepper
2 courgettes, trimmed
1 small aubergine, trimmed
1 onion, peeled
2 ripe tomatoes
50 g/2 oz button
mushrooms, wiped and halved
or quartered
200 ml/7 fl oz tomato juice
1 tbsp freshly chopped basil
salt and freshly ground
black pepper

Deseed the pepper, remove the membrane with a small, sharp knife and cut into small dice. Thickly slice the courgettes and cut the aubergine into small dice. Slice the onion into rings.

Place the tomatoes in boiling water until their skins begin to peel away. Remove the skins from the tomatoes, cut into quarters and remove the seeds.

Place all the vegetables in the cooking dish with the tomato juice and basil. Season to taste with salt and pepper. Cover with the lid and switch the slow cooker to auto. Cook for 1½ hours, or until tender but still retaining a bite, *al dente*. Remove the vegetables with a slotted spoon and arrange in a serving dish.

Pour the liquid into a saucepan and bring to the boil. Boil for 20 seconds until it is slightly thickened. Season the sauce to taste with salt and pepper. Pass the sauce through a sieve to remove some of the seeds and pour over the vegetables. Serve the ratatouille hot or cold.

Mixed Vegetable Curry

Serves 4–6

2 tbsp vegetable oil
1 tsp cumin seeds
1 tsp black mustard seeds
2–3 garlic cloves, peeled
and chopped
1 tbsp hot curry powder
2 onions, peeled and cut
into wedges
225 g/8 oz sweet potatoes,
peeled and chopped
225 g/8 oz potatoes, peeled
and chopped
175 g/6 oz carrots, peeled
and chopped
175 g/6 oz cauliflower florets
300 ml/½ pint water
125 g/4 oz frozen peas, thawed
3 tomatoes, chopped
few fresh curry leaves, chopped
2 tbsp ground almonds
4 tbsp natural yogurt
1 tbsp freshly chopped coriander,
to garnish

Heat the oil in a large frying pan, add the seeds and fry for 30 seconds, or until they pop.

Add the garlic, curry powder and onions and cook gently for 5 minutes, or until the onions have softened.

Add the remaining vegetables, except for the peas and tomatoes, to the pan. Add the water, bring to the boil, then carefully transfer to the cooking dish. Cover with the lid and switch the slow cooker to auto. Cook for 1 hour, then switch the slow cooker to low and cook for 5 hours.

Add the peas and tomatoes and continue to cook on low for 1 hour. Stir in the curry leaves, ground almonds and yogurt. Continue to cook on low for 30 minutes, or until hot. Garnish with chopped coriander and serve.

Red Lentil Kedgeree

Serves 4

150 g/5 oz easy-cook basmati rice
150 g/5 oz red lentils
15 g/¹⁄₂ oz butter
1 tbsp sunflower oil
1 medium onion, peeled
and chopped
1 tsp ground cumin
4 cardamom pods, bruised
1 bay leaf
450 ml/³⁄₄ pint vegetable stock
1 ripe avocado, peeled,
stoned and diced
1 tbsp lemon juice
4 plum tomatoes, peeled and diced
2 tbsp freshly chopped coriander
salt and freshly ground
black pepper
lemon or lime slices, to garnish

Put the rice and lentils in a sieve and rinse under cold running water. Tip into a bowl, then pour over enough cold water to cover and leave to soak for 10 minutes.

Heat the butter and oil in a saucepan. Add the sliced onion and cook gently, stirring occasionally, for 10 minutes until softened. Stir in the cumin, cardamom pods and bay leaf and cook for a further minute, stirring all the time.

Drain the rice and lentils, rinse again and add to the onions in the saucepan. Stir in the vegetable stock and bring to the boil. Transfer to the cooking dish and cover with the lid. Switch the slow cooker to auto and cook for 1 hour. Switch the cooker to low and cook for 4–5 hours until the rice and lentils are tender.

Place the diced avocado in a bowl and toss with the lemon juice. Stir in the tomatoes and chopped coriander. Season to taste with salt and pepper.

Fluff up the rice with a fork, spoon into a warmed serving dish and spoon the avocado mixture on top. Garnish with lemon or lime slices and serve.

Vegetable ❧ Lentil Casserole

Serves 4

225 g/8 oz Puy lentils
1–2 tbsp olive oil
1 onion, peeled and chopped
2–3 garlic cloves, peeled
and crushed
300 g/11 oz carrots, peeled
and sliced into chunks
3 celery stalks, trimmed
and sliced
350 g/12 oz butternut squash, peeled,
seeds removed and diced
1 litre/1¾ pints vegetable stock
salt and freshly ground
black pepper
few fresh oregano sprigs, plus
extra to garnish
1 large red pepper, deseeded
and chopped
2 courgettes, trimmed and sliced
150 ml/¼ pint sour cream,
to serve

Pour the lentils out onto a plate and look through them for any small stones, then rinse the lentils and reserve.

Heat the oil in a deep frying pan, add the onion, garlic, carrots and celery and sauté for 5 minutes, stirring occasionally.

Add the squash and lentils. Pour in the stock and season to taste with salt and pepper. Add the oregano sprigs and bring to the boil.

Carefully transfer to the cooking dish and cover with the lid. Switch the slow cooker to low and cook for 6 hours.

Add the red pepper and courgettes and stir. Continue to cook for a further 1–2 hours until all the vegetables are tender. Adjust the seasoning, garnish with sprigs of fresh oregano and serve with sour cream.

Pastini-stuffed Peppers

Serves 6

6 red, yellow or orange peppers,
tops cut off and deseeded
salt and freshly ground
black pepper
175 g/6 oz small pasta shells
or shapes
4 tbsp olive oil
1 onion, peeled and finely chopped
2 garlic cloves, peeled and
finely chopped
3 ripe plum tomatoes, skinned,
deseeded and chopped
50 ml/2 fl oz dry white wine
8 pitted black olives, chopped
4 tbsp freshly chopped mixed herbs, such
as parsley, basil, oregano or marjoram
125 g/4 oz mozzarella
cheese, diced
4 tbsp grated Parmesan cheese
fresh tomato sauce, preferably
home-made, to serve

Bring a pan of water to the boil. Trim the bottom of each pepper so it sits upright. Blanch the peppers for 2–3 minutes, then drain on absorbent kitchen paper. Return the water to the boil, add 1/2 teaspoon salt and the pasta and cook for 3–4 minutes until *al dente*. Drain thoroughly, reserving the water. Rinse under cold running water, drain again and reserve.

Heat 2 tablespoons of the olive oil in a large frying pan, add the onion and cook for 3–4 minutes. Add the garlic and cook for 1 minute. Stir in the tomatoes and wine and cook for 5 minutes, stirring frequently. Add the olives, herbs, mozzarella cheese and half the Parmesan cheese. Season to taste with salt and pepper. Remove from the heat and stir in the pasta.

Dry the insides of the peppers with absorbent kitchen paper, then season lightly. Arrange the peppers in the lightly oiled cooking dish and fill with the pasta mixture. Sprinkle with the remaining Parmesan cheese and drizzle over the remaining oil. Pour in 150 ml/1/4 pint boiling water. Switch the slow cooker to high and cook for 45 minutes, or until the peppers are tender. Serve immediately with freshly made tomato sauce.

Vegetable ❧ Coconut Pot

Serves 4–6

2 tbsp vegetable oil or ghee
1 tsp cumin seeds
1 cinnamon stick, bruised
3 whole cloves
3 cardamom pods, bruised
1/2–1 tsp chilli powder
8 shallots, peeled and halved
2–3 garlic cloves, peeled
and finely chopped
225 g/8 oz potatoes, peeled
and cut into chunks
about 350 g/12 oz butternut squash,
peeled, deseeded, cut into chunks
225 g/8 oz carrots, peeled
and chopped
200 ml/7 fl oz water
300 ml/1/2 pint coconut milk
225 g/8 oz French beans, trimmed
and chopped
400 g/14 oz can red kidney beans,
drained and rinsed
4–6 spring onions, trimmed
and finely chopped

Heat the oil or ghee in a large saucepan, add the seeds, cinnamon stick, cloves, cardamom pods and chilli powder and fry for 30 seconds, or until the seeds pop.

Add the shallots, garlic, potatoes, squash and carrots and stir until the vegetables are coated in the flavoured oil. Add the water, bring to the boil, then carefully transfer to the cooking dish. Cover with the lid.

Switch the slow cooker to low and cook for 6 hours. Pour in the coconut milk and add the chopped beans and kidney beans, then stir gently until thoroughly mixed together.

Continue to cook for a further 2 hours, or until the vegetables are tender. Sprinkle with the chopped spring onions and serve.

Delicious

Desserts

The benefits of the slow cooker are endless! In this chapter, you'll quickly learn how to make perfectly moist Carrot Cake, or Gingerbread for that nostalgic Christmassy feeling. But the possibilities don't end there; try the Chocolate Rice Pudding or Chocolate and Fruit Crumble for a decadent mix of fruity and spicy flavours, or opt for the Golden Castle Pudding for a sweet sticky indulgence.

Bramley Apple Cake

Cuts into 8 slices

175 g/6 oz self-raising flour
1 tsp baking powder
175 g/6 oz unsalted
butter, softened
175 g/6 oz caster sugar, plus
extra for sprinkling
1 tsp vanilla extract
3 medium eggs, beaten
450 g/1 lb Bramley cooking apples, peeled,
cored and sliced
1 tbsp lemon juice
1/2 tsp ground cinnamon
fresh custard sauce or cream,
to serve

Lightly oil and line the base of an 18 cm/7 inch, deep cake tin with baking paper. Place an upturned saucer or trivet in the cooking dish and pour in 2.5 cm/1 inch cold water. Switch the slow cooker to high.

Sift the flour and baking powder into a small bowl. Beat the butter, sugar and vanilla extract until light and fluffy. Gradually beat in the eggs a little at a time. Stir in the flour, adding a little cooled boiled water, to give a dropping consistency. Spoon about one third of the mixture into the tin, smoothing the surface.

Toss the apple slices into the lemon juice and cinnamon and spoon over the cake mixture, making an even layer. Spread the remaining mixture over the apple layer to the edge of the tin, making sure the apples are covered.

Smooth the top with the back of a wet spoon and sprinkle with sugar. Place in the cooking dish and cover with oiled foil. Pour in boiling water to halfway up the sides of the tin. Cover with the lid and cook in the slow cooker for 4–6 hours. Remove from the slow cooker; cool for at least 30 minutes. Run a knife blade between the cake and the tin to loosen the cake and invert onto a rack. Discard the lining paper. Turn the cake the right way up to cool. Serve with custard sauce or cream.

Rhubarb Crumble

Serves 6

125 g/4 oz plain flour
50 g/2 oz softened butter
50 g/2 oz rolled oats
50 g/2 oz demerara sugar
1 tbsp sesame seeds
1/2 tsp ground cinnamon
450 g/1 lb fresh rhubarb
50 g/2 oz caster sugar
custard or cream, to serve

Lightly oil a 900 ml/1 1/2 pint, heatproof dish. Place an upturned saucer or trivet in the base of the cooking dish, pour round 2.5 cm/1 inch cold water and switch the cooker to high.

Place the flour in a large bowl and cut the butter into cubes. Add to the flour and rub in until the mixture looks like fine breadcrumbs, or blend for a few seconds in a food processor. Stir in the rolled oats, demerara sugar, sesame seeds and cinnamon. Mix well and reserve. Prepare the rhubarb by removing the thick ends of the stalks and cut diagonally into 2.5 cm/1 inch chunks. Wash thoroughly and pat dry with a tea towel.

Place the rhubarb in the serving dish. Sprinkle the caster sugar over the rhubarb and top with the reserved crumble mixture. Level the top of the crumble and press down firmly. If liked, sprinkle the top with caster sugar. Cover with an oiled sheet of foil, then place in the slow cooker. Pour round boiling water to halfway up the sides.

Cook for 4–6 hours until the fruit is tender. If a crisp topping is preferred, remove the foil for the last 30–45 minutes of cooking time. If liked, sprinkle the pudding with some more caster sugar and serve hot with custard or cream.

Topsy Turvy Pudding

Serves 6

For the topping
175 g/6 oz demerara sugar
2 medium oranges

For the sponge
175 g/6 oz butter, softened
175 g/6 oz caster sugar
3 medium eggs, beaten
175 g/6 oz self-raising
flour, sifted
50 g/2 oz plain dark
chocolate, melted
grated zest of 1 orange
25 g/1 oz cocoa powder, sifted, plus
extra for dusting
custard or sour cream, to serve

Place the demerara sugar and 3 tablespoons water in a saucepan and heat gently until the sugar dissolves, then boil until a golden caramel is formed. Pour into the base of an 18 cm/7 inch, deep cake tin and leave to cool for 2–3 minutes. Swirl the caramel round the sides of the tin until coated. Reserve. Place an upturned saucer or trivet in the cooking dish and pour in 2.5 cm/1 inch water. Switch the cooker to high.

Cream the butter and sugar together. Beat in the eggs a little at a time, adding flour after each addition. Add the melted chocolate; stir well. Fold in the orange zest, the remaining flour, sifted cocoa powder and 1–2 tablespoons cooled boiled water. Mix well to give a soft dropping consistency.

Remove the peel from both oranges. Slice the peel into strips, then slice the oranges. Arrange the peel and orange slices over the caramel. Top with the chocolate mixture and level the top. Cover with a pleated sheet of foil brushed with oil. Place the tin in the cooking dish and pour round boiling water to come halfway up the sides.

Cover with the lid and cook for 4–6 hours until the top feels firm. Remove from the slow cooker, invert onto a serving plate and sprinkle with cocoa powder. Serve with either custard or sour cream.

Poached Pears

Serves 4

2 small cinnamon sticks
125 g/4 oz caster sugar
300 ml/¹/₂ pint red wine
150 ml/¹/₄ pint water
thinly pared zest and juice of
1 small orange
4 firm pears
orange slices, to decorate
frozen vanilla yogurt, or ice cream, to serve

Place the cinnamon sticks on the work surface and, with a rolling pin, slowly roll down the side of the cinnamon sticks to bruise. Place in the cooking dish.

Add the sugar, wine, water, pared orange zest and juice to the cooking dish and switch the slow cooker to low. Cover with the lid and cook for 1 hour, stirring occasionally.

Meanwhile, peel the pears, leaving the stalks intact.

Cut out the cores from the bottoms of the pears and level them so that they will stand upright in the serving dish.

Sit the pears in the syrup in the cooking dish, re-cover and continue to cook on low. Cook for 4–6 hours until the pears are tender.

Switch the slow cooker off and leave the pears to cool in the syrup, turning occasionally.

Arrange the pears on serving plates and spoon over the syrup. Decorate with the orange slices and serve with the yogurt or ice cream and any remaining juices.

Chestnut Cake

č

Serves 6

100 g/3¹/₂ oz butter, softened
100 g/3¹/₂ oz caster sugar
100 g/3¹/₂ oz canned sweetened chestnut purée
2 medium eggs, lightly beaten
100 g/3¹/₂ oz self-raising flour
1 tsp baking powder
pinch ground cloves
1 tsp fennel seeds, crushed
50 g/2 oz raisins
25 g/1 oz pine nuts, toasted
125 g/4 oz icing sugar
5 tbsp lemon juice
pared strips lemon rind, to decorate

Oil and line an 18 cm/7 inch, deep cake tin. Place an upturned saucer or trivet in the cooking dish and pour in 2.5 cm/1 inch cold water. Switch the slow cooker to high. Beat together the butter and sugar. Beat in the chestnut purée. Gradually add the eggs, beating after each addition. Sift in the flour with the baking powder and cloves. Add the fennel seeds and beat. The mixture should drop easily from a wooden spoon when tapped against the side of the bowl. If not, add a little milk.

Stir in the raisins and pine nuts. Spoon the mixture into the tin and smooth. Cover with a sheet of lightly oiled foil. Place in the cooking dish. Pour in boiling water to halfway up the sides of the tin. Cover with the lid and cook on high for 4–6 hours until a skewer inserted in the centre of the cake comes out clean.

Remove from the slow cooker and let cool in the tin while preparing the syrup. Mix together the icing sugar and lemon juice in a small saucepan until smooth. Heat gently, but do not boil. Using a cocktail stick or skewer, make holes all over the cake. Pour the syrup evenly over the cake and leave to soak in.

Leave until cool before removing from the tin and discarding the lining paper. Decorate with the strips of lemon rind.

Carrot Cake

Cuts into 8–10 slices

175 g/6 oz self-raising flour
1 tsp baking powder
1 tsp ground cinnamon
1/2 tsp ground ginger
150 g/5 oz dark soft brown sugar
100 g/3 1/2 oz butter
2 medium eggs, beaten
1 tbsp vanilla extract
2 carrots, peeled and grated (about 175 g/6 oz peeled weight)
125 g/4 oz pecans or walnuts, toasted and chopped
50 g/2 oz ground almonds

For the frosting

175 g/6 oz cream cheese, softened
50 g/2 oz butter, softened
1 tsp vanilla extract
225 g/8 oz icing sugar, sifted
1–2 tbsp milk

Lightly oil and line the base of an 18 cm/7 inch, deep cake tin with baking paper and dust the base with a little flour. Place an upturned saucer or trivet in the cooking dish and pour in 2.5 cm/1 inch cold water. Switch the slow cooker to high.

Sift the flour, baking powder and spices into a mixing bowl and stir in the sugar. Add the butter and rub in until the mixture resembles fine breadcrumbs, then make a well in the centre. Beat the eggs with the vanilla extract and pour into the well. Mix together; stir in the carrots, chopped nuts and ground almonds.

Spoon into the tin and smooth the surface. Place on the saucer and pour in sufficient boiling water to come halfway up the sides. Cover with a piece of lightly oiled foil. Cook for 4–6 hours until firm and a skewer inserted into the centre comes out clean.

Remove from the slow cooker and leave to cool before removing from the tin and discarding the lining paper. For the frosting, beat the cream cheese, butter and vanilla extract together until smooth, then gradually beat in the icing sugar until the frosting is smooth. Spread the frosting over the top. Refrigerate for about 1 hour to set the frosting, then cut into squares and serve.

Sweet-stewed Dried Fruits

Serves 4

500 g/1 lb 2 oz packet mixed
dried fruit salad
450 ml/¾ pint apple juice
2 tbsp clear honey
2 tbsp brandy
1 lemon
1 orange

To decorate
crème fraîche
fine strips pared
orange zest

Place the fruits, apple juice, clear honey and brandy in a saucepan.

Using a small, sharp knife or a zester, carefully remove the zest from the lemon and orange and place in the pan.

Squeeze the juice from the lemon and orange and add to the pan.

Bring the fruit mixture to the boil, then carefully transfer to the cooking dish. Cover with the lid and switch the slow cooker to low. Cook for 6–8 hours. Switch the cooker off and allow to rest for 30 minutes.

Transfer the mixture to a large bowl, cover with clingfilm and chill in the refrigerator overnight to allow the flavours to blend.

Spoon the stewed fruit into four shallow dessert dishes. Decorate with a large spoonful of crème fraîche and a few strips of the pared orange zest and serve.

Chocolate & Fruit Crumble

Serves 4

For the crumble
125 g/4 oz plain flour
125 g/4 oz butter
75 g/3 oz soft light brown sugar
50 g/2 oz rolled porridge oats
50 g/2 oz hazelnuts, chopped

For the filling
450 g/1 lb Bramley apples
1 tbsp lemon juice
50 g/2 oz sultanas
50 g/2 oz seedless raisins
50 g/2 oz soft light
brown sugar
350 g/12 oz pears, peeled,
cored and chopped
1 tsp ground cinnamon
125 g/4 oz plain dark chocolate, very
roughly chopped
2 tsp caster sugar, for sprinkling

Lightly oil an ovenproof dish that will sit comfortably in the cooking dish. Place an upturned saucer or trivet into the dish and pour round 2.5 cm/1 inch cold water. Switch the slow cooker to high. For the crumble, sift the flour into a large bowl. Cut the butter into small cubes and add to the flour. Rub the butter into the flour. Stir in the sugar, porridge oats and chopped hazelnuts and reserve.

For the filling, peel the apples, core and slice. Place in a heavy-based saucepan with the lemon juice and 3 tablespoons water. Add the sultanas, raisins and soft brown sugar. Bring to the boil, cover and simmer over a gentle heat for 8–10 minutes, stirring occasionally, until the apples are slightly softened.

Remove the saucepan from the heat and leave to cool slightly before stirring in the pears, ground cinnamon and chopped chocolate. Spoon into the prepared dish. Sprinkle the crumble evenly over the top and place in the cooking dish. Cover with a sheet of oiled foil. Pour round boiling water to halfway up the sides. Cover with the lid and cook in the slow cooker for 4–5 hours until the top is golden.

Remove the foil for the last 30 minutes of cooking to crisp the top. Remove from the cooker, sprinkle with caster sugar and serve.

Chocolate Rice Pudding

Serves 4

150 g/5 oz pudding rice
50 g/2 oz caster sugar
410 g can evaporated milk
600–900 ml/1–1½ pints milk
pinch freshly grated nutmeg
¼ tsp ground cinnamon (optional)
50 g/2 oz plain chocolate chips
freshly sliced strawberries,
to decorate
crème fraîche, to serve

Lightly butter the cooking dish. Switch the slow cooker to high. Rinse the pudding rice, then place in the base of the buttered cooking dish and sprinkle over the caster sugar.

Pour the evaporated milk and 600 ml/1 pint of the milk into a heavy-based saucepan and bring slowly to the boil over a low heat, stirring occasionally to avoid sticking. Pour the milk over the rice and sugar and stir well.

Grate a little nutmeg over the top, then sprinkle with the ground cinnamon, if using. Cook on high in the slow cooker for 3–4 hours, or on low for 6–8 hours.

Stir occasionally during cooking in order to break up any lumps. Add more milk if necessary.

Stir the chocolate chips into the rice pudding. Continue to cook uncovered for a further 30 minutes, or until the rice is tender. Serve warm, with or without the skin, according to personal preference. Serve with a few sliced strawberries and a spoonful of crème fraîche.

Gingerbread

Cuts into 8 slices

225 g/8 oz butter
125 g/4 oz black treacle
125 g/4 oz dark muscovado sugar
350 g/12 oz self-raising flour
2–3 tsp, or to taste, ground ginger
2 tbsp milk
2 medium eggs
1 tsp stem ginger syrup
1–2 pieces stem ginger in syrup

Lightly oil and line the base of an 18 cm/7 inch, deep, round cake tin with greaseproof or baking paper. Place an upturned saucer or trivet in the cooking dish and pour in 2.5 cm/1 inch cold water. Switch the slow cooker to high.

In a saucepan, gently heat the butter, black treacle and sugar, stirring occasionally, until the butter melts. Leave to cool slightly.

Sift the flour and ground ginger into a large bowl. Make a well in the centre, then pour in the treacle mixture. Add the milk and stir lightly together.

Beat the eggs, then stir into the mixture. Beat the mixture until well mixed and free of lumps. Pour into the prepared tin and place in the cooking dish. Cover with a piece of lightly oiled foil. Cover with the lid and cook in the slow cooker for 4–6 hours until well risen and a skewer inserted into the centre comes out clean.

Carefully remove from the slow cooker and allow to cool in the tin, then remove and discard the lining paper. Pour the syrup over the top of the cake. Slice the stem ginger into thin slivers and sprinkle over the cake. Serve.

Eve's Pudding

Serves 6

450 g/1 lb cooking apples
175 g/6 oz blackberries
75 g/3 oz demerara sugar
grated zest of 1 lemon
125 g/4 oz caster sugar
125 g/4 oz butter
few drops vanilla extract
2 medium eggs, beaten
125 g/4 oz self-raising flour
1 tbsp icing sugar
ready-made custard, to serve

Lightly oil a 900 ml/1½ pint ovenproof dish that will fit in the cooking dish. Place an upturned saucer or trivet into the dish and pour round 2.5 cm/1 inch cold water. Switch the slow cooker to high.

Peel, core and slice the apples and place a layer in the base of the prepared dish. Sprinkle over some of the blackberries, a little demerara sugar and lemon zest. Continue to layer the apple and blackberries until all the ingredients have been used. Cream the sugar and butter together until light and fluffy.

Beat in the vanilla extract and then the eggs a little at a time, adding a spoonful of flour after each addition. Fold in the extra flour and mix well. Spread the sponge mixture over the top of the fruit and level with the back of a spoon. Cover tightly with an oiled piece of foil. Place the dish in the cooking dish and pour round sufficient water to come halfway up the sides.

Cover with the lid and cook in the slow cooker for 4–6 hours until well risen and golden brown. (To test if the pudding is cooked, press the cooked sponge lightly with a clean finger – if it springs back, the sponge is cooked.) Dust the pudding with a little icing sugar and serve immediately with custard.

Chocolate Buttermilk Cake

Cuts into 8 slices

125 g/4 oz butter
1 tsp vanilla extract
125 g/4 oz caster sugar
2 medium eggs, separated
100 g/3$^{1}/_{2}$ oz self-raising flour
25 g/1 oz cocoa powder
125 ml/4 fl oz buttermilk

For the icing

200 g/7 oz plain dark chocolate
100 g/3$^{1}/_{2}$ oz butter
150 ml/$^{1}/_{4}$ pint double cream

Oil and line the base of an 18 cm/7 inch, deep cake tin with baking paper. Place an upturned saucer or trivet in the cooking dish and pour in 2.5 cm/1 inch cold water. Switch the slow cooker to high.

Cream together the butter, vanilla extract and sugar, then beat in the egg yolks one at a time. Sift together the flour and cocoa powder and fold into the egg mixture with the buttermilk. Whisk the egg whites and fold carefully into the cocoa mixture in two batches. Spoon the mixture into the tin and cover with oiled foil.

Place in the cooking dish and pour round boiling water to halfway up the sides. Cover with the lid and cook in the slow cooker for 4–6 hours until firm. Cool slightly, then remove from the slow cooker and leave to cool for 30 minutes.

Turn onto a wire rack and let cool before discarding the lining paper. Melt the chocolate and butter together in a heatproof bowl set over simmering water. Stir until smooth, then leave at room temperature until the chocolate is spreadable. Split the cake horizontally in half. Use some of the chocolate mixture to sandwich the two halves together. Spread and decorate the top of the cake with the remaining chocolate mixture. Finally, whip the cream and spread around the cake. Refrigerate until required. Serve cut into slices. Refrigerate to store.

Golden Castle Pudding

ỡ

Serves 4–6

125 g/4 oz butter
125 g/4 oz caster sugar
few drops vanilla extract
2 medium eggs, beaten
125 g/4 oz self-raising flour
4 tbsp golden syrup
crème fraîche or ready-made
custard, to serve

Lightly oil 4–6 150 ml/¼ pint individual pudding bowls and place a small circle of lightly oiled nonstick baking or greaseproof paper in the base of each one. Place a trivet or metal pastry cutter with a flat plate on top into the cooking dish and pour round 2.5 cm/1 inch cold water. Switch the slow cooker to high.

Place the butter and caster sugar in a large bowl, then beat together. Stir in the vanilla extract and add the eggs, a little at a time. Add a tablespoon flour after each addition of egg and beat well. When the mixture is smooth, add the remaining flour and fold in. Add a tablespoon water and mix to drop easily off a spoon. Spoon enough mixture into each basin to come halfway up the tin, allowing enough space for rising.

Cover with a double sheet of oiled foil and place on the plate. Pour round boiling water to halfway up the sides of the pudding basins. Cover with the lid and cook in the slow cooker for 3–4 hours.

Remove from the slow cooker and allow the puddings to stand for 5 minutes. Turn out onto individual serving plates and discard the greaseproof paper circles. Warm the golden syrup in a small saucepan and pour a little over each pudding. Serve hot with the crème fraîche or custard.

Lemon Drizzle Cake

ℰ

Cuts into 16 squares

125 g/4 oz unsalted butter
or margarine
125 g/4 oz caster sugar
2 medium eggs
125 g/4 oz self-raising flour
2 lemons, preferably unwaxed
50 g/2 oz granulated sugar

Oil and line the base of an 18 cm/7 inch, deep cake tin with baking paper. Place an upturned saucer or trivet in the cooking dish and pour in 2.5 cm/1 inch cold water. Switch the slow cooker to high. In a large bowl, cream the butter or margarine and sugar together. Beat the eggs, then gradually add a little of the egg to the mixture, adding 1 tablespoon flour after each addition. Grate the zest from one of the lemons and stir into the creamed mixture, beating well until smooth. Squeeze the juice from the lemon, strain, then stir in.

Spoon into the tin, then level. Place in the cooking dish and pour in boiling water to halfway up the sides of the tin. Cover with a piece of oiled foil. Cover with the lid and cook in the slow cooker for 4–6 hours.

Remove from the cooker. Using a zester, remove the peel from the last lemon and mix with 25 g/1 oz of the sugar and reserve. Squeeze the juice from the lemon into a small saucepan. Add the rest of the granulated sugar and heat gently, stirring. When the sugar has dissolved, simmer for 3–4 minutes. With a cocktail stick, prick the cake all over. Sprinkle the lemon zest and sugar over the top of the cake, drizzle over the syrup and leave to cool. Discard the lining paper before cutting the cake into squares and serving.

Stuffed Amaretti Peaches

Serves 4

4 ripe peaches
grated zest and juice of 1 lemon
50 g/2 oz amaretti biscuits
25 g/1 oz chopped blanched
almonds, toasted
25 g/1 oz pine nuts, toasted
40 g/1 1/2 oz light muscovado sugar
25 g/1 oz butter
1 medium egg yolk
6 tbsp lemon or orange juice
2 tsp clear honey (optional)
crème fraîche or Greek yogurt,
to serve

Halve the peaches and remove the stones. Take a very thin slice from the bottom of each peach half so that it will sit flat in the cooking dish. Dip the peach halves in lemon juice and place in a dish that will fit in the cooking dish.

Crush the amaretti biscuits and put into a mixing bowl. Add the almonds, pine nuts, sugar, lemon zest and butter. Work with the fingertips until the mixture resembles coarse breadcrumbs. Add the egg yolk and mix well until the mixture just comes together.

Divide the amaretti and nut mixture between the peach halves, pressing down lightly. Place in the cooking dish and pour round the lemon or orange juice, then cover with a pleated sheet of foil and then the lid.

Switch the slow cooker to low and cook for 4–5 hours until the peaches are tender. Remove the foil for the last 30 minutes of cooking time. Remove the peaches from the slow cooker and drizzle with the honey, if using.

Place two peach halves on each serving plate and spoon over a little crème fraîche or Greek yogurt, then serve.

College Pudding

❦

Serves 4

75 g/3 oz shredded suet
75 g/3 oz fresh white breadcrumbs
50 g/2 oz sultanas
50 g/2 oz seedless raisins
$1/2$ tsp ground cinnamon
$1/4$ tsp freshly grated nutmeg
$1/4$ tsp mixed spice
40 g/$1 1/2$ oz caster sugar
$1/2$ tsp baking powder
2 small eggs, beaten
orange zest, to garnish

Lightly oil a 600 ml/1 pint pudding basin and place a small circle of greaseproof paper in the base. Place an upturned saucer or trivet into the cooking dish and pour round 2.5 cm/1 inch cold water. Switch the slow cooker to high.

Mix the shredded suet and breadcrumbs together and rub lightly with the fingertips to remove any lumps.

Stir in the dried fruit, spices, sugar and baking powder. Add the eggs and beat lightly together until the mixture is well blended and the fruit is evenly distributed. Spoon the mixture into the prepared pudding basin and level the surface. Cover with a lightly oiled pleated sheet of foil. Tuck the foil securely round the rim of the dish.

Place in the slow cooker and pour round sufficient boiling water to come halfway up the sides of the basin. Cover with the lid and cook for 4–5 hours. Remove the foil and continue to cook for 1 hour, or until the top is firm.

When the pudding is cooked, carefully remove from the cooker and leave to cool for 5–10 minutes. Turn out onto a warmed serving dish and discard the lining paper. Decorate with the orange zest and serve immediately.

Index

A